Daily Discoveries
for January

Thematic Learning Activities for
EVERY DAY

Written by Elizabeth Cole Midgley
Illustrated by Jennette Guymon-King

Teaching & Learning Company

1204 Buchanan St., P.O. Box 10
Carthage, IL 62321-0010

This book belongs to

_____

Several of the activities in this book involve preparing, tasting and sharing food items. We urge you to be aware of any food allergies or restrictions your students may have and to supervise these activities diligently. All food-related suggestions are identified with this allergy-alert symbol: ⚠

Please note: small food items (candies, raisins, cereal, etc.) can also pose a choking hazard.

Cover art by Jennette Guymon-King

Copyright © 2005, Teaching & Learning Company

ISBN No. 1-57310-466-3

Printing No. 987654321

Teaching & Learning Company
1204 Buchanan St., P.O. Box 10
Carthage, IL 62321-0010

At the time of publication every effort was made to insure the accuracy of the information included in this book. However, we cannot guarantee that agencies and organizations mentioned will continue to operate or maintain these current locations.

Table of Contents

Dear Teacher or Parent,

Due to the stimulus of a high-tech world, parents and teachers are often faced with the challenge of how to capture the attention of a child and create an atmosphere of meaningful learning opportunities. Often we search for new ways to meet this challenge and help young people transfer their knowledge, skills and experiences from one area to another. Subjects taught in isolation can leave a feeling of fragmentation. More and more educators are looking for ways to be able to integrate curriculum so that their students can fully understand how things relate to each other.

The Daily Discoveries series has been developed to that end. The premise behind this series has been, in part, the author's educational philosophy: anything can be taught and absorbed by others in a meaningful way, depending upon its presentation.

In this series, each day has been researched around the history of a specific individual or event and has been developed into a celebration or theme with integrated curriculum areas. In this approach to learning students draw from their own experience and understanding of things, to a level of processing new information and skills.

The Daily Discoveries series is an almanac-of-sorts, 12 books (one for each month) that present a thematically based curriculum for grades K-6. The series contains hundreds and hundreds of resources and ideas that can be a natural springboard to learning. These ideas have been used in the classroom and at home, and are fun as well as educationally sound. The activities have been endorsed by professors, teachers, parents and, best of all, by children.

The Daily Discoveries series can be used in the following ways for school or home:
- to develop new skills and reinforce previous learning
- to create a sense of fun and celebration every day
- as tutoring resources
- as enrichment activities that can be used as time allows
- for family fun activities

Sincerely,

Elizabeth

Elizabeth Cole Midgley

New Year's Day

January 1

Setting the Stage

- Display a picture of a giant wishing well (gray construction paper "stones" for the base and a brown construction paper "tile" well "roof"). A gold construction paper "bell" can be hung under the center of the roof. Use the caption: "Here's Wishing You WELL This Coming Year!" Students can write on construction paper water pails about their hopes for the New Year. These pails can be displayed around the well.

- If you live in a cooler area, use this bulletin board idea. Display a picture of students in winter clothing (coats, scarves and mittens) surrounded by book jacket covers. Add the caption: "Warm Up to a Good Book!"

- Construct a semantic map or web with what your students already know about New Year's Day and its customs. Students can share questions they have during the course of the day.

New
Year's
Day

New
Year's
Day

New
Year's
Day

CELEBRATE THE NEW YEAR

Setting the Stage continued

• Add colorful (blown-up) balloons with streamers or curling ribbon dangling from each one to the top of a bulletin board. Add the caption: "Celebrate the New Year!" Underneath, display student New Year's resolutions. See reproducible for New Year's resolutions on page 12 and "Writing Experience" on page 12.

Historical Background

New Year's Day is a public holiday in the United States and other countries. January 1 is the first day of the first month in the Gregorian calendar year.

Literary Exploration

Class Clown by Johanna Hurwitz
Happy New Year! by Emily Kelley
New Year's Poems by Myra Cohn Livingston
We Celebrate New Year by Bobbie Kalman

Language Experience

• Brainstorm together New Year's Day customs and traditions that students have with their families.

Writing Experience

• Let students write their New Year's resolutions. Younger children might need help in understanding what goals are and deciding how they can make improvements in certain areas of their life. Display resolutions on a bulletin board.

• Students will enjoy guessing what family members and friends might wish or hope for in the New Year. Some students might want to write what they think a famous person's New Year's goals or hopes might be.

• Challenge students to reflect on highlights of the past year and write about them. See reproducible on page 13.

Science/Health Experience

- What are some goals people might have (global goals) in order to have a healthier life or planet?

Social Studies Experience

- Research New Year's Eve customs around the world. How did they begin? How are they different and similar? Example: In the Orient, children celebrate their birthdays on this day. People receive new clothes, decorate their homes and pay off debts they have incurred during the past year. In Japan, bells ring 108 times (a way to get rid of evil).

Music/Dramatic Experience

- Students might want to "interview" others around the school about their New Year's resolutions.

Physical/Sensory Experience

- Procure store-bought or handmade noise-makers (such as pots and pans or pie-tin tambourines to bang on). Have your own New Year's parade around your school or classroom.

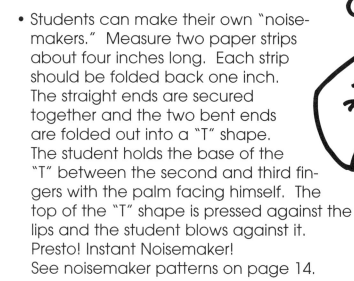

- Students can make their own "noise-makers." Measure two paper strips about four inches long. Each strip should be folded back one inch. The straight ends are secured together and the two bent ends are folded out into a "T" shape. The student holds the base of the "T" between the second and third fingers with the palm facing himself. The top of the "T" shape is pressed against the lips and the student blows against it. Presto! Instant Noisemaker! See noisemaker patterns on page 14.

- Remember the icons of Father Time and the new-born baby? Blindfold one child at a time and play Pin the Diaper on the Baby as you would play Pin the Tail on the Donkey. They must place the diaper pin on the X, or as close to it as possible. See patterns on page 15.

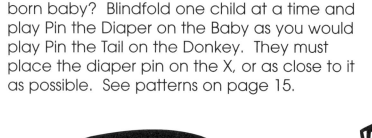

Arts/Crafts Experience

- Make New Year's hats! Students form cone shapes from construction paper and add glitter, sequins, buttons and bows, etc., to make zany hats. A cluster of yarn can be a tassel for a final touch! See decoration patterns on page 16.

HAPPY NEW YEAR

- New Year bells can be made out of construction paper and corn syrup. Students trace and cut out bell shapes from heavy construction paper. Each bell is drizzled with white corn syrup. Children can choose three different colors of food coloring to drop in three separate areas on their bell. They spread the syrup all over the bell (being careful not to mix any of the colors together). When the entire bell is covered, it needs to be set aside to dry for a few days. Once dry, it takes on a colorful shiny luster and makes a beautiful display!

- Ring in the New Year with beautiful silver bells! Provide each student with two paper cups, a foot of aluminum foil and a foot-long piece of thin ribbon. Students cut the ribbon in half, then poke a hole in the bottom of each cup and thread half the ribbon into the hole. They cut the aluminum foil in half and cover the outside of each cup (setting aside two small pieces of aluminum foil). They pull the ribbon inside the cup partway and wrap a small piece of aluminum foil (in a ball shape) around the bottom of the ribbon for the "clapper" that dangles and rings, inside the bell. The other bell is made the same way, then they can tie the tops of the two ribbons together in a bow.

Extension Activities

• How about making a time capsule? Brainstorm and collect items that seem to typify the year as it is coming in (or each student's goals) and store them in a shoe box to hide until the end of the school year. Be sure and make a note of where it is hidden and when to bring it forth so it can be shown at the appropriate time.

⚠ In Greece, a special cake (peta) is baked with a coin inside to bring luck for the coming year. Put foil-covered chocolate coins inside "Good-Luck Cupcakes."

Follow-Up/Homework Idea

• Encourage students to begin one thing towards the realization of one of their New Year's goals.

Remembering the best of **LAST YEAR**

Name: _____

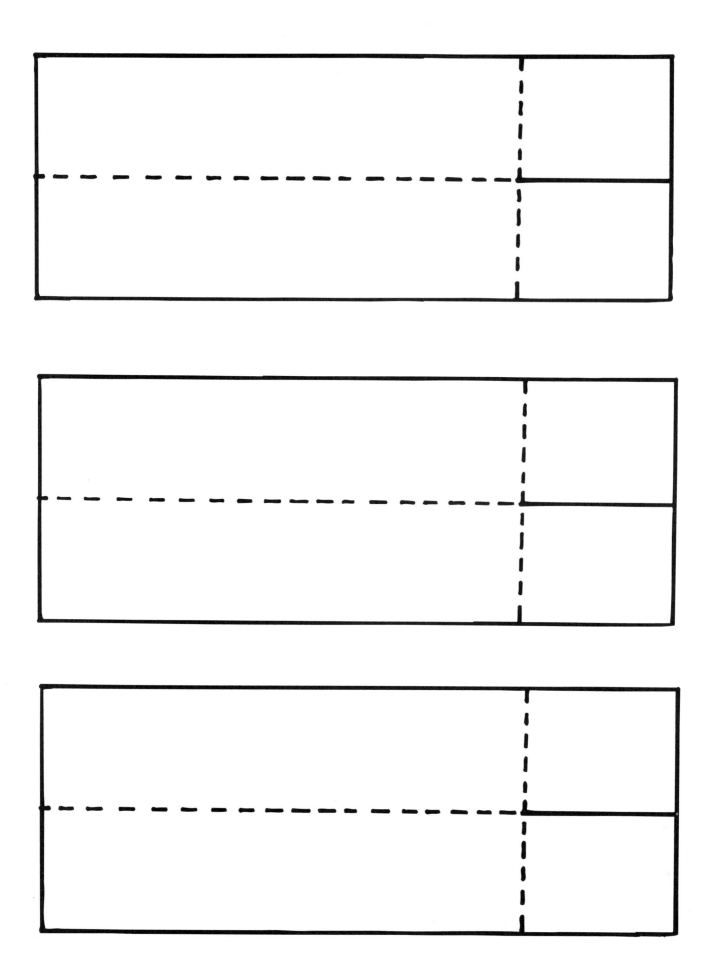

Cut out baby,
glue on poster board and
laminate for durability.
Cut out baby pins (outside only)
and laminate. Apply a small piece
of rolled tape to the back of each
baby pin and see who can get the closest to
the X while blindfolded.

16

Soup Day

January 2

Setting the Stage

• Have a "souper" day and warm up your students at the same time! Display all kinds of soup cans on a table. Cook up a crockpot of favorite soup and let your students smell the aroma of soup cooking while they work throughout the day! Challenge them to solve this riddle: "What has 26 letters but is not in the alphabet?" (alphabet soup)

• Construct a semantic map or web on the board with facts the students already know about soup. Then ask them to write questions about soup they would like answered.

Historical Background

Back in the old days, soup was considered a meal in itself. The very first restaurant is believed to have been opened by a Parisian soup vendor in 1765. January has been designated National Soup Month by the Campbell® Soup Company.

Literary Exploration

Alphabet Soup by Kate Banks
Alphabet Soup: A Feast of Letters by Scott Gustafson
Bear Sleep Soup by Jasper Tomkins
Blue Moon Soup Spoon by Mimi Otey
Chicken Soup with Rice: A Book of Months by Maurice Sendak
Chicken Soup, Boots by Maira Kalman
Doodle Soup by John Ciardi
Dumpling Soup by Jama Kim Rattigan
Famous Seaweed Soup by Antoinette Truglio Martin
Fish and Soup: A Fish Tale by Susan Sully
Full Moon Soup: Or the Fall of the Hotel Splendide by Alastair Graham
George and Martha by James Marshall
Group Soup by Barbara Brenner
Growing Vegetable Soup by Lois Ehlert
Ice Cream Soup by Frank Modell
Ice Cream Soup by Gail Herman
Lentil Soup by Joe Lasker
Little Boy Soup by David L. Harrison
Martha Calling by Susan Meddaugh
Mean Soup by Betsy Everitt
"Me-Stew" a poem from *Where the Sidewalk Ends* by Shel Silverstein
Monkey Soup by Louis Sachar
Moon Soup by Lisa Desimini
Mouse Soup by Arnold Lobel
Nail Soup: A Swedish Folktale by Harve Zemach
Pea Soup and Sea Serpents by William Schroder
Riddle Soup by Valiska Gregory
Simon's Soup by Beverly Komoda
Soup (series) by Robert Newton Peck
Soup for Supper by Phyllis Root
Stone Soup by Marcia Brown
Stone Soup by Ann McGovern
Stone Soup by Tony Ross
The Runaway Soup and Other Stories by Michael Muntean
The Soup Bone by Tony Johnston
Tomato Soup by Edith Thacher Hurd
Turnip Soup by Lynne and Christopher Myers
"Turtle Soup" a poem by Lewis Carroll
Uncle Willie and the Soup Kitchen by DyAnne DiSalvo-Ryan
Vegetable Soup by Jeanne Modesitt
Watch Out for the Chicken Feet in Your Soup! by Tomie dePaola
Yuck! by James Stevenson

Soup Day

Soup Day

Soup Day

TLC10466 Copyright © Teaching & Learning Company, Carthage, IL 62321-0010

Language Experience

- Alphabet soup can be what you make it! Give students 10 vocabulary words that need to be arranged in alphabetical order, or scramble letters from a spelling list and challenge students to figure out the words and spell them correctly. See reproducible on page 22.

Writing Experience

- Explain to students that they are going to open up a new soup restaurant. They need to write a menu with soup descriptions and prices.

- Have students write their favorite soup recipes. They can write the ingredients on shopping lists and the recipes on recipe cards. See patterns on page 23.

Math Experience

• Make a large graph to show the amounts and kinds of soup eaten by students' families during the month of January. They can bring soup can labels to glue to the graph to keep an accurate record all month.

Science/Health Experience

• This is a good opportunity to teach students how to read and examine the nutritional label on cans. Teach them where to look for fat grams and calories on products. Explore which of the soups have the most fat or highest amount of sodium.

Social Studies Experience

• After reading *Uncle Willie and the Soup Kitchen* by DyAnne DiSalvo-Ryan, discuss the important work that goes on in soup kitchens throughout the world to help those who are less fortunate. Invite someone who works (or has worked) in a soup kitchen to share his or her experiences with the class. Your class may wish to begin a canned soup drive to help support a local soup kitchen.

TLC10466 Copyright © Teaching & Learning Company, Carthage, IL 62321-0010

Music/Dramatic Experience

⚠ Read *Stone Soup* (by several authors listed on page 18) Pick one your class would like to act out. Have students bring ingredients from home and add your own (sterilized) stone and water. The culminating activity is, of course, eating some delicious stone soup!

- Divide students into cooperative groups to write jingles or advertisements for new kinds of soup.

- People used to eat soup as a main dish. Challenge students to give short speeches on the merits of soup standing alone as a main dish. Other students may point out the problems of this plan.

Arts/Crafts Experience

- Allow students a chance to design new can labels for their favorite soups.

Extension Activities

⚠ Have a soup-sampling party! Invite students to bring their favorite soups to share with one another. Serve crackers with the soup samples.

- Is there a soup kitchen in your area you could get permission to visit? If your class could spend time serving soup to others, it could be a powerful lesson in empathy!

Values Education Experience

- Give each student a chance to stand up front while everyone "brags" about why that student is such a "soup"er student and why he or she is a valued member of the class! See award patterns on page 24.

I'm "Souper" because...

Follow-Up/Homework Idea

- Encourage students to go home and enjoy their favorite soup for dinner!

TLC10466 Copyright © Teaching & Learning Company, Carthage, IL 62321-0010

J.R.R. Tolkien's Birthday

January 3

Setting the Stage

• Celebrate the whimsical world of fantasy today! Encourage students to leave the world of the ordinary behind and let their imaginations go wild! Attach butcher paper to a wall or table and let students "doodle" their ideas wherever their imaginations take them.

• Construct a semantic map or web of words your students associate with the term *fantasy*.

Historical Background

John Ronald Reuel Tolkien, a famous English writer, was born on this day in 1892. He is known for his trilogy, *Lord of the Rings* and *The Hobbitt*.

Literary Exploration

The Case of the Dragon in Distress by E.W. Hildick
Chronicles of Narnia by C.S. Lewis
The Forgotten Door by Alexander Key
The Grey King by Susan Cooper
I Spy Fantasy by Jean Marzollo
Peter Pan by James Barrie
The Prydain (series) by Lloyd Alexander
Tuck Everlasting by Natalie Babbitt
The Wonder Ring: A Fantasy in Silhouette by Holden Wetherbee

Language Experience

• Review the idea of reality vs. fantasy. Create a Venn diagram of the similarities and differences.

Writing Experience

• Challenge students to write short stories (or paragraphs) to "stump" the readers (rest of the class) with their validity. Invite students to read their stories aloud and let the class guess which are true and which are fantasy. See reproducible on page 28.

Math Experience

• Take a poll to find out students' favorite fantasy books and show the results on a classroom graph.

Music/Dramatic Experience

- Divide students into cooperative groups to write fantasy scripts and act them out in front of your class or another class.

- Let students debate the issue of fantasy vs. reality-based literature. Is one more important than the other or is there merit in both types?

Extension Activities

- Remember the television series *Fantasy Island*? Invite students to divide into groups and create their own "fantasy islands." Each group needs to decide on food, shelter, supplies, occupations, monetary system and resources needed to live independently on an island. They will explain their plans to the rest of the class.

⚠ For a fun treat, whip up tropical fruits and whipped cream (or ice cream) to make "Fantasy Floats!"

Arts/Crafts Experience

- If your students create their "fantasy islands" (above), let them create models of their islands. Using boxes, construction paper, toilet paper tubes, etc.

Values Education Experience

- Discuss the idea of "escaping" through good literature or inspiring music into "another world." Discuss how such "escapes" help us with our daily lives.

Follow-Up/Homework Idea

- Encourage students to go to the library and check out fantasy-based books to begin reading on their own.

Grimms' Fairy Tale Day

January 4

Grimms'
Fairy
Tale

Grimms'
Fairy
Tale

Grimms'
Fairy
Tale

Setting the Stage

- Get into "character" by dressing up as one of your favorite fairy tale personalities and invite your students to do the same. Possibilities include: king or queen, Cinderella, wolf, Prince Charming, woodsman, dragon or knight.

- On a bulletin board, display a fairy tale castle on a layer of white cotton batting clouds. Add glitter for a spectacular display.

- Create a fairy "wand" from a ruler with a construction paper star stuck on one end. Use the wand throughout the day to tap desks of students to line up first, to answer questions, etc.

- Now that Christmas is over, you can buy gingerbread house kits for very little. Make one in your class for Hansel and Gretel's candy house in the forest.

- Construct a semantic map or web with facts your students already know about fairy tales (or would like to know) to help you structure the emphasis and activities of the day.

Historical Background

Of the brothers Grimm, Jacob, was born on this day in 1785. He and his brother, Wilhelm Karl, were famous for their folklore. Although they had previously studied law, they were enchanted with stories that had been handed down orally for generations. The Grimm brothers decided to write these stories down so they wouldn't be lost through time. Children everywhere have loved these tales for many years.

Literary Exploration

Beauty and the Beast by Jan Brett
Beauty: A Retelling of the Story of Beauty and the Beast by Robin Mckinley
The Bremen Town Musicians by Brothers Grimm
Briar Rose by Jane Yolen
The Child's Fairy Tale Book by Kay Chorao
Cinderella by Peter Elwell
Cinderella by Barbara Karlin
Cinderella by Charles Perrault and Amy Ehrlich
Dragonwings by Laurence Yep
Each Peach Pear Plum by Janet and Allan Ahlberg
A Fairy Tale by Tony Ross
The Fairy Tale Cookbook by Carol MacGregor
The Fairy Tale Treasury by Raymond Briggs
The Fisherman and His Wife by Jacob and Wilhelm Grimm
The Frog Prince by Gerda Neubacher
The Frog Prince Continued by Jon Scieszka
Grimm's Fairy Tales by Jacob Grimm
Hansel and Gretel by Jacob and Wilhelm Grimm
Hansel and Gretel retold by Rika Lesser
Jack and the Beanstalk by Steven Kellogg
The Juniper Tree and Other Tales from Grimm by Jacob and Wilhelm Grimm
King Grisley Beard by Jacob and Wilhelm Grimm
Kiss a Frog! Jokes About Fairy Tales, Knights and Dragons by Rick and Ann Walton
Knights of the Kitchen Table by Jon Scieszka
Lon Po Po: A Red-Riding Hood Story from China by Ed Young
Paper Bag Princess by Robert Munsch
Pinocchio by Carlo Collodi, et al
Princess Furball by Charlotte Huck
Read Me a Fairy Tale by Rose Impey
Rindercella by Archie Campbell
Rumpelstiltskin by Jacob and Wilhelm Grimm
Sleeping Ugly by Jane Yolen
Snow White and the Seven Dwarfs by Jacob and Wilhelm Grimm
The Snow Queen by Hans Christian Andersen
Saint George and the Dragon retold by Margaret Hodges
Three Little Pigs and the Big Bad Wolf by Glen Rounds
The Twelve Dancing Princesses by Jacob and Wilhelm Grimm
Thorn Rose by Brothers Grimm

Grimms' Fairy Tale

TLC10466 Copyright © Teaching & Learning Company, Carthage, IL 62321-0010

Language Experience

• Learn about fairy tales as a literary genre.

• Read the classic version of *Cinderella* (titles listed on page 30) and *Princess Furball* by Charlotte Huck. Make a class Venn diagram showing their similarities and differences.

• Try and stump your class by posing riddles about fairy tale characters or playing Twenty Questions with "yes" and "no" answers.

Writing Experience

• If your students could trade places with any fairy tale character, who would it be and why? Have them write their answers.

• Teach students how to write a fairy tale by reviewing the elements that usually make up a standard fairy tale. Most fairy tales begin with "Once upon a time . . ." or "There once was a . . ." They end with "And they all lived happily ever after." The story usually takes place in an Old World setting such as a kingdom or castle, or a in a village or forest. There is often an unexpected hero or heroine and usually some repetition of story lines or a predictable pattern. Numbers are often involved, such as seven dwarfs or three guesses. A journey or quest with a lesson usually ends with good triumphing over evil. Have each student write an original fairy tale on the reproducible on page 35.

Math Experience

• Let students take a survey at recess or lunchtime of students' favorite fairy tales. They can tally the results and add their findings on a class bar graph. You may want to give students some fairy tales to choose from.

Science/Health Experience

• Toss some lima beans out a window (as Jack did) and discuss whether or not the beans will grow. Talk about the requirements for a seed to take root and grow into a healthy, surviving plant.

Social Studies Experience

• Encourage students to check out fairy tales from around the world at a local library and notice their differences and similarities.

TLC10466 Copyright © Teaching & Learning Company, Carthage, IL 62321-0010

Music/Dramatic Experience

• Challenge some students to act out some of the jokes from *Kiss a Frog! Jokes About Fairy Tales, Knights and Dragons* by Rick and Ann Walton.

• Divide students into cooperative groups to act out or pantomime their favorite fairy tales.

Physical/Sensory Experience

• Play Catch the Dragon's Tail! Students line up holding onto the shoulders of the person in front of them. The last person hangs a bandanna (or piece of red crepe paper) out of a back pocket. The head of the dragon (front person) tries to "catch" the tail (bandanna) without anyone in line letting go.

Grimms'
Fairy
Tale

Grimms'
Fairy
Tale

Arts/Crafts Experience

• Decide together which fairy tales your students would like to illustrate. Then make a *Giant Fairy Tale Book!* Divide into cooperative groups with each group in charge of illustrating (in bright, vivid color) a major scene of their fairy tale on card stock or poster board. Punch holes in the edge of all the illustrations. Bind them together with heavy cord. Add a cover and a title. Students can take turns "telling" and "re-telling" their favorite fairy tales with the book. It will make a great addition to one of your classroom centers for browsing for the rest of the school year.

• Students can make their own fire-breathing dragons. Give each a green plastic cup with a hole poked in the bottom. Have them tape thin paper streamers or ribbon inside the cup. A craft stick can be glued to the bottom of the cup for a handle. After the stick is dry and fastened securely, students can glue two green pompoms (for eyes) with wiggly eye centers on the cup. They can blow into the hole and make the streamers wave as the dragon "breathes."

Extension Activities

• Pick a favorite recipe from *The Fairy Tale Cookbook* and try it out as a class!

Values Education Experience

• In many classic fairy tales, some people are unjustly treated and yet respond in kindness. Discuss the value of kindness and its impact on inspiring others.

Follow-Up/Homework Idea

• Invite students to read a favorite fairy tale to a younger brother or sister (or teddy bear).

Once Upon a time...

By:

George Washington Carver Day

January 5

George
Washington
Carver

Setting the Stage

- Display books about George Washington Carver. Gather agricultural by-products (items Carver worked on) such as: soap, cosmetics, cheese, paint, ink, wood dyes or kitty litter. Display the items to stimulate interest in today's study.

- Construct a semantic map or web with facts your students know about peanuts. Let them list a few questions they have about peanuts or about Dr. George Washington Carver. Try to answer them during the course of the day.

Historical Background

George Washington Carver was a botanist and teacher who did important work with crops. Many farmers in the South were dealing with crop failure. After many years of growing cotton, the soil was becoming depleted of oxygen. Carver encouraged farmers to use alternative crops (peanuts, sweet potatoes, soybeans) to restore nitrogen to the soil. His agricultural study included developing uses for these crops so farmers would continue planting them. Carver was born a slave and his birth date is unknown, though it's said to be sometime in 1864 or 1865. He died on this day in 1943. He left all his life's savings to the George Washington Carver Foundation for continued research in his beloved field of agriculture. His headstone reads: "He could have added fortune to fame, but caring for neither, he found happiness and honor in being helpful to the world."

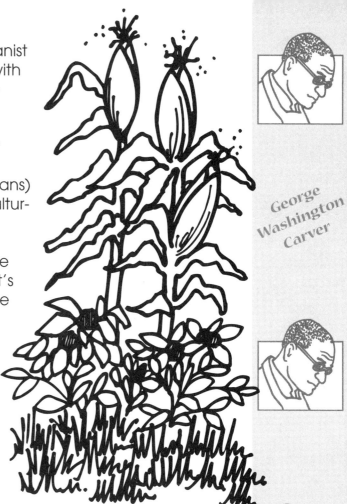

George Washington Carver

Literary Exploration

George Washington Carver by Gene Adair
George Washington Carver by Suzanne Coil
George Washington Carver by Sam and Beryl Epstein
George Washington Carver by James Marion Gray
George Washington Carver by Lois Nicholson
George Washington Carver by Anne Terry White
George Washington Carver: In His Own Words by George Washington Carver, edited by Gary R. Kremer
George Washington Carver: Nature's Trailblazer by Teresa Rogers
George Washington Carver: Negro Scientist by Sam and Beryl Epstein
George Washington Carver: The Peanut Scientist by Patricia and Fredrick McKissack
Make Me a Peanut Butter Sandwich and a Glass of Milk by Ken Robbins
Outward Dreams: Black Inventors and Their Inventions by Jim Haskins
Peanut Butter and Jelly by Nadine Bernard Westcott
"Peanut Butter Sandwich" a poem from *Where the Sidewalk Ends* by Shel Silverstein
A Pocketful of Goobers: A Story of George Washington Carver by Barbara Mitchell
The Story of George Washington Carver by Eva Moore
A Weed Is a Flower: The Life of George Washington Carver by Aliki

George Washington Carver

George Washington Carver

Language Experience

- Cut a large piece of newspaper in a peanut shape and title it "News in a Nutshell!" Let students write world and local news reports on cards and mount them on the peanut.

Writing Experience

- Let students write directions for a recipe using sweet potatoes or peanuts.

- Ask students if they ever think of themselves as "nuts." Let them write about experiences when they realized they were acting nuts! See reproducible on page 42.

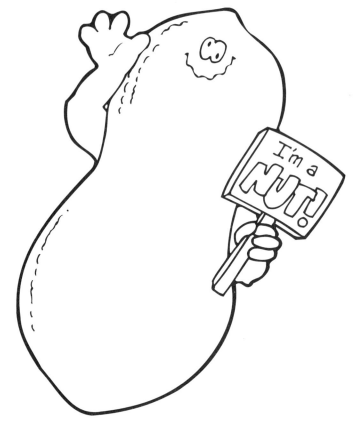

Math Experience

- Poll students to discover their preference for smooth or chunky peanut butter. Show the results on a class graph. Make a graph showing other things that taste good with peanut butter besides jelly.

- Let students try to estimate the amount of peanuts in a jar or guess how many peanuts it would take to go across each desk.

- This is a good opportunity to review addition or subtraction skills with peanuts (in shells) for counters.

Science/Health Experience

- Grow sweet potato plants! Place a sweet potato in a clear plastic cup 3/4 full of water. Support the potato with toothpicks and place the cup in a sunny window. Watch the roots grow!

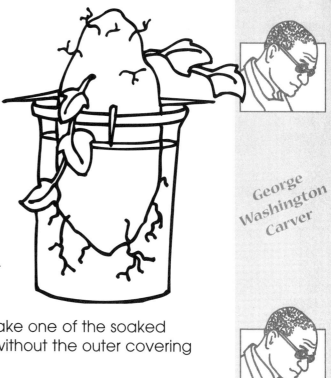

- Study the science of peanuts. Did you know that peanuts are not nuts, but legumes? Research together the difference between a peanut and a nut. To find out how peanuts grow underground, start your own peanut plant. Soak raw peanuts overnight, then plant a few about an inch deep in sandy soil. Keep the soil moist and watch for a sprout within a week. Students can take one of the soaked peanuts apart to see what it looks like without the outer covering before it is planted.

Social Studies Experience

- George Washington Carver invented more than 300 different by-products or uses for the sweet potato and the peanut. Let your class research some of the products he developed.

Music/Dramatic Experience

- Sing the song, "Peanut Butter" with your students. Add verses for spreading the peanut butter, picking the grapes for jelly, etc. On the last verse students just hum the tune because the peanut butter is sticking their mouths together!

"Peanut, Peanut Butter, Jelly
Peanut, Peanut Butter, Jelly
First, you take the peanuts
and you dig'em, you dig'em
You dig'em, dig'em dig'em!

Peanut, Peanut Butter, Jelly
Peanut, Peanut Butter, Jelly
Next, you take the peanuts
and you smash'em, you smash'em
You smash'em, smash'em smash'em!

Physical/Sensory Experience

- Have a Peanut-on-a-Spoon Relay or hide peanuts (in the shell) for a scavenger hunt.

- Play a Peanut Butter and Jelly ball game. Students form a circle and begin passing a ball (peanut butter) in a given direction. Add another ball (jelly) a few seconds later. The object is for students to try and catch the second ball with the first one. When this is done, everyone yells, "Peanut Butter and Jelly." Then the process begins again.

Arts/Crafts Experience

⚠ Make edible Peanut Butter Play Dough!

Peanut Butter Play Dough
1 cup creamy peanut butter
1 cup light corn syrup
1/4 cup non-fat dry milk
1/4 cup powdered sugar

Mix together and knead slightly. The mixture is very gooey, but fun to sculpt with and delicious to eat!

Extension Activities

⚠ Try making homemade peanut butter. Blend 1 cup of unsalted peanuts and 1/2 teaspoon of salt with 3 tablespoons of oil in a blender. Or let students snack on fresh peanuts!

⚠ Serve Peanut Butter Ritz Bits™ or Nutter Butter Bites™ for a fun treat!

⚠ Your students will love making yummy peanut butter treats. For Peanut Butter Pizza, make a favorite pizza crust (or use English muffins). Top with peanut butter mixed with honey. Then add raisins, banana slices or whatever they want.

No-Bake Peanut Butter Cookies

1 c. oatmeal

1 c. non-fat dry milk

1/2 c. peanut butter

1/2 c. honey

Mix together and press into
a 9 x 12 pan or shape into balls.
Chill and serve!

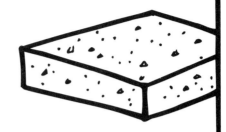

Homemade Peanut Butter Cups

1 quart jar peanut butter

1 cake paraffin wax

1 lb. margarine

2 boxes powdered sugar

3 pkgs. chocolate chips

Melt margarine, add peanut butter and sugar. Mix well. Shape
into balls the size of walnuts. Melt paraffin and chocolate chips.
Dip balls into chocolate. Place on wax paper. Makes about 100 balls.

Values Education Experience
• Discuss what Carver might have meant when he said, "No man can
drag me down so low as to make me hate him."

Follow-Up/Homework Idea
• Encourage each student to make up a new recipe for a familiar
vegetable!

George
Washington
Carver

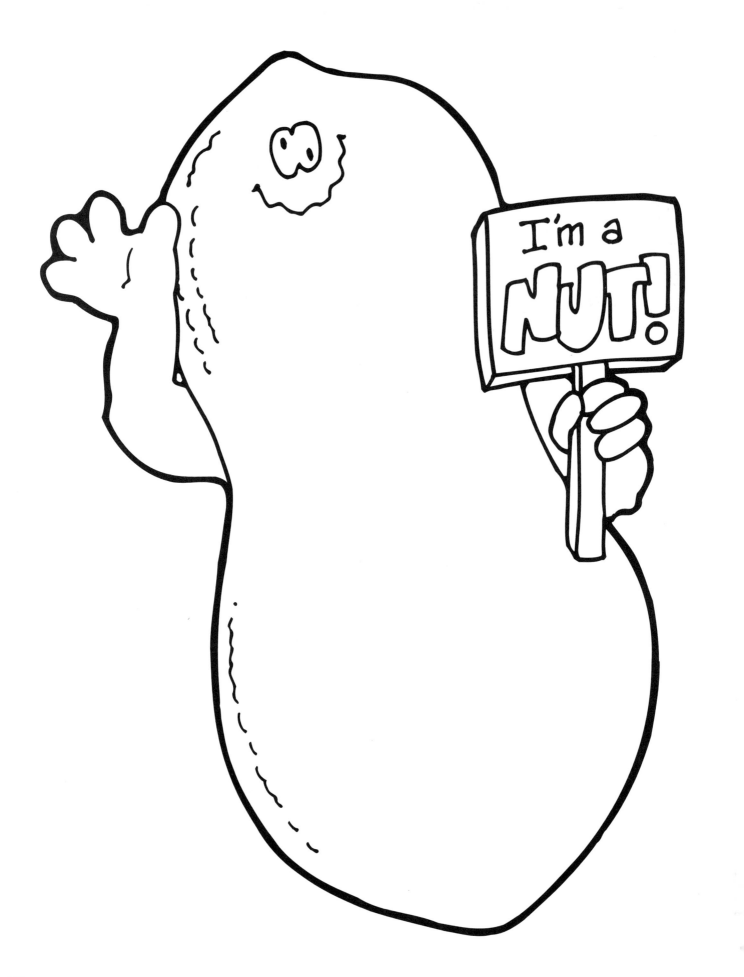

New Mexico Statehood Day

January 6

Setting the Stage

- Construct a semantic map or web with facts your students already know (or would like to know) about the state of New Mexico.

Historical Background

New Mexico became the 47th state to join the United States on this day in 1912.

Literary Exploration

America, the Beautiful: New Mexico by Conrad Stein
New Mexico by John Allan Carpenter
New Mexico by Judith Bloom Fradin
New Mexico by Kathleen Thompson

Language Experience

• Create a class Venn diagram of Old Mexico (the country) and New Mexico (the state) pointing out the similarities and differences.

• Brainstorm together other states that have *new* in their names There are three others.

Writing Experience

• New Mexico joins three other states to form "The Four Corners" (Utah, Colorado, Arizona and New Mexico). Let students guess where these states are and write what they know about the other three states. Then check on a map to see who is right.

Science/Health Experience

• Learn about cactus and why they grow abundantly in New Mexico. What conditions help them to prosper? Learn about how cactus grow, then grow a class cactus to take care of and observe.

Social Studies Experience

• Learn about New Mexico and its people. What things are unique to the state of New Mexico? What are its state symbols, products and special places of interest?

44

Physical/Sensory Experience

- Play Statue Cactus. Students need a play area where they can run around for this game. They run around and at a signal (such as a whistle) they must freeze in the shape of a cactus. If, someone moves before they are allowed to unfreeze, that person is out of the game. The game continues with running and freezing, as students are eliminated from the game one by one.

- Play Four Corner Ball. On a blacktop area which has four squares that are touching, have one student stand in each square. One of the students is captain. The captain bounces a ball into a square. The student in that square receives the ball, catching it before it bounces twice. If it bounces more than once or rolls, that student is out and another takes that place. The idea is to keep the ball bouncing once in every square without eliminating students. If a blacktop area with four square markings is not available, use masking tape to make squares on the floor.

Arts/Crafts Experience

- Have students make New Mexico flags using its original flag colors.

- Students can make salt-dough relief maps of New Mexico.

Extension Activities

⚠ Make an "edible cactus." Make your favorite crisp rice cereal treat recipe and let students shape it into small cactuses. Small pieces of stick pretzels can be added for a final touch.

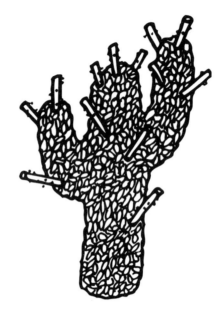

⚠ The pinion is New Mexico's state tree. How about serving Pinion pine nuts as a treat?

• Invite students or their parents to share experiences in New Mexico or artifacts found there. Many Indian reservations are found there and people may have Native American crafts or jewelry from visits to this great state.

Follow-Up/Homework Idea

• The roadrunner is the New Mexico state bird. Have students watch for "Roadrunner" cartoons and look for the roadrunner's features (such as speed or feather colors).

Magnificent Mittens Day

January 7

Setting the Stage

• Burr! It's that time of the year in many places to bundle up in a coat and slip on cozy mittens. Today is Magnificent Mittens Day! Display a variety of colors, sizes and fabrics of mittens. Check at a local thrift store for inexpensive mittens to display.

• Invite students to wear and bring in all the mittens they can "get their hands on" for today's activities. Label each mitten with a name on masking tape to identify them later.

Setting the Stage continued

- Display mitten shapes on a bulletin board. On each mitten, write a fast finisher activity such as: "List everything you can think of that is very cold." Display the completed mittens on a bulletin board with the caption: "Warm up with these cozy activities!" See medium mitten patterns on page 53.

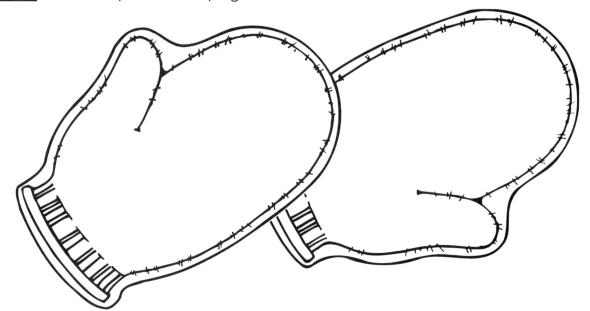

- Construct a semantic map or web with facts your students already know (or would like to know) about mittens to help you structure the day's activities.

- Let students graph the mittens you have gathered today.

Literary Exploration

Caps, Hats, Socks and Mittens by Louise Borden
A Kitten in My Mitten by JoAnne Nelson
The Mitten by Alvin Tresselt
The Mitten: A Ukrainian Folktale by Jan Brett
Mitten/Kitten by Jerome Martin
Mittens by Clare Turlay Newberry
The Mystery of the Missing Red Mitten by Steven Kellogg
One Mitten Lewis by Helen Kay
Red Mittens by Laura May Bannon
Runaway Mittens by Jean Rogers
Three Little Kittens Lost Their Mittens by Elaine Livermore
Too Many Mittens by Florence Slobodkin
The Woodcutter's Mitten by Loek Koopmans

Magnificent Mittens

Language Experience

- Create a class Venn diagram showing the similarities and differences between a mitten and a glove.

- Have students write a contraction, antonym (or whatever you are currently studying) on one mitten and a correct match on another mitten. Then they mix them up and try to locate matches. The correct answers may be pinned up on a class "clothesline" to be taken down and mixed up again and again by fast finishers throughout the day. See small mittens patterns on page 54.

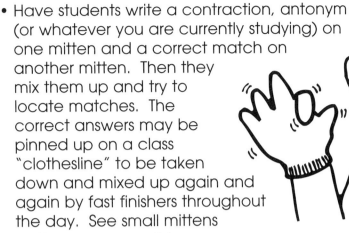

Writing Experience

- Sample story starters for today:

    If you could choose to be too cold or too hot, what would you choose and why?

    One cold day a . . . .

    It was really hard but we finally found the lost mitten. It had . . . The mitten must have been magic because . . .

    I didn't know it but I had been frozen for ten years and . . .

    See large mitten pattern on page 55.

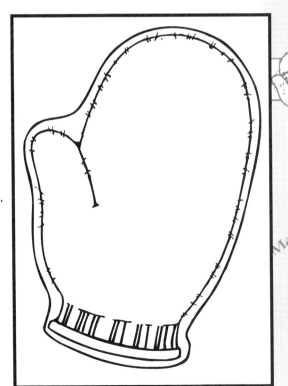

Math Experience

• Make Math Mittens. Let each student trace a mitten pattern and write a sum on it, then trace another mitten and write on it a math problem to fit the sum. Example: 18 on a mitten and 9 + 9 on another. Students bring all their mittens to a designated area to be mixed up. Use them for a class math relay game or at a math center. See small mitten patterns on page 54.

• Challenge students to figure out the rough area and perimeter of a pair of mittens.

• Let students graph mittens according to color, size and design on a large class bar graph.

• Reinforce the concept of counting by twos by counting the pairs of mittens.

Science/Health Experience

• Conduct some science experiments with gloves and mittens. Are some materials water repellent? When holding an ice cube, which seems to keep the cold out better—gloves or mittens?

Social Studies Experience

• Use a map or globe, to point out areas of the world where people would probably NOT need gloves or mittens. Discuss areas such as those near the equator and other temperate areas around the globe.

Music/Dramatic Experience

• After reading *Three Little Kittens Lost Their Mittens* by Elaine Livermore, let students take turns acting out the parts of the Three Little Kittens.

Physical/Sensory Experience

• Have students try on both gloves and mittens. Why does one let you move your fingers and the other does not? What are the advantages and disadvantages of each?

• Play Mitten, Mitten . . . Who's Got the Mitten? Students sit in a circle with one student in the middle. A single mitten is passed behind their backs while they close their eyes. On a signal, students open their eyes and the student in the middle of the circle tries to guess who has the mitten. If the guess is correct, they exchange places and the game continues.

• Mix up the mittens and gloves, separating the pairs, and reinforce the concept of one-to-one correspondence by challenging students to go on a scavenger hunt to find matching pairs.

Arts/Crafts Experience

• Let students trace two mitten patterns on felt and cut them out. Let them use a heavy-duty hole punch to punch holes all around the outside of both mittens, then "sew" yarn through the holes to secure the mittens together. They can decorate their mittens with glitter, sequins, lace, rickrack or whatever you have on hand.

Extension Activities

• Gloves and mittens are always in big demand during cold months at homeless shelters. Call a representative from a homeless shelter to come to your class so students can donate their extra gloves and mittens.

⚠ Serve snowball-shaped cupcakes, found in most grocery stores, for a tasty treat (with or without mittens)!

Follow-Up/Homework Idea

• For a homework assignment, ask students to do a family service project. Each can go around the house making sure all mittens and gloves are clean, matched up correctly and in a special place for family members to use when needed. If your students do not live in a place where mittens are needed, they can always do the same with "feet mittens" (socks)!

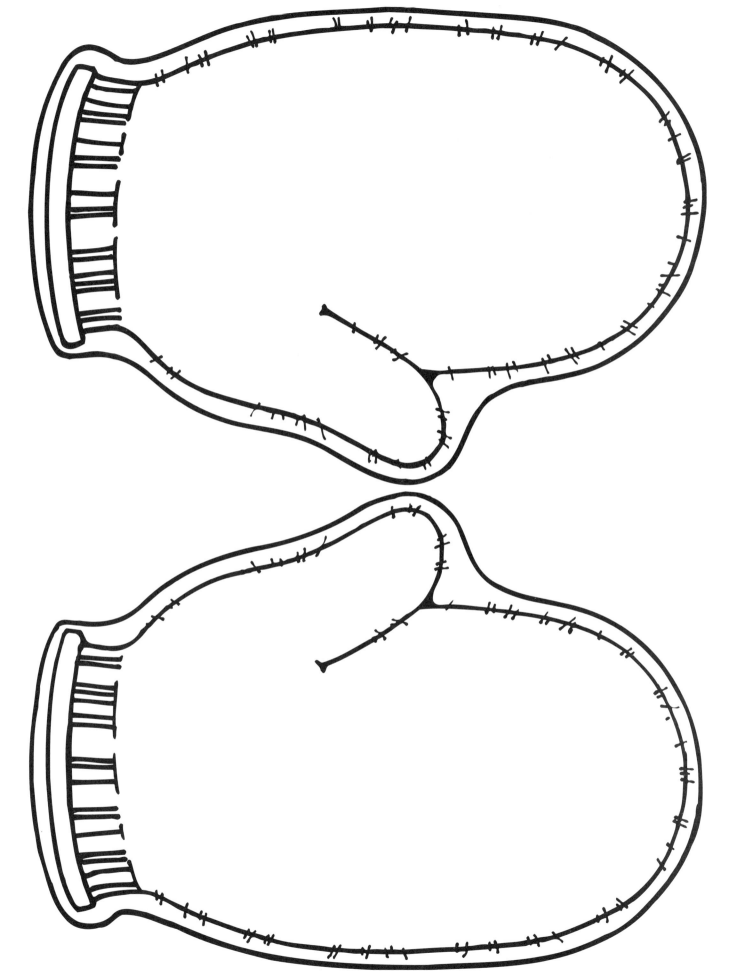

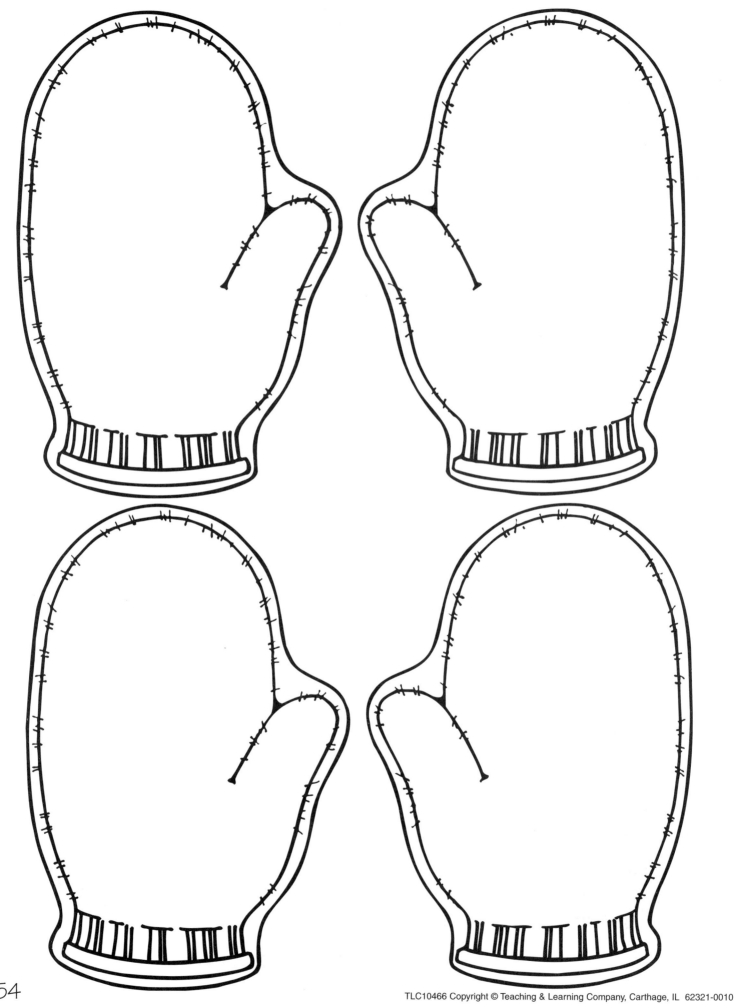

54

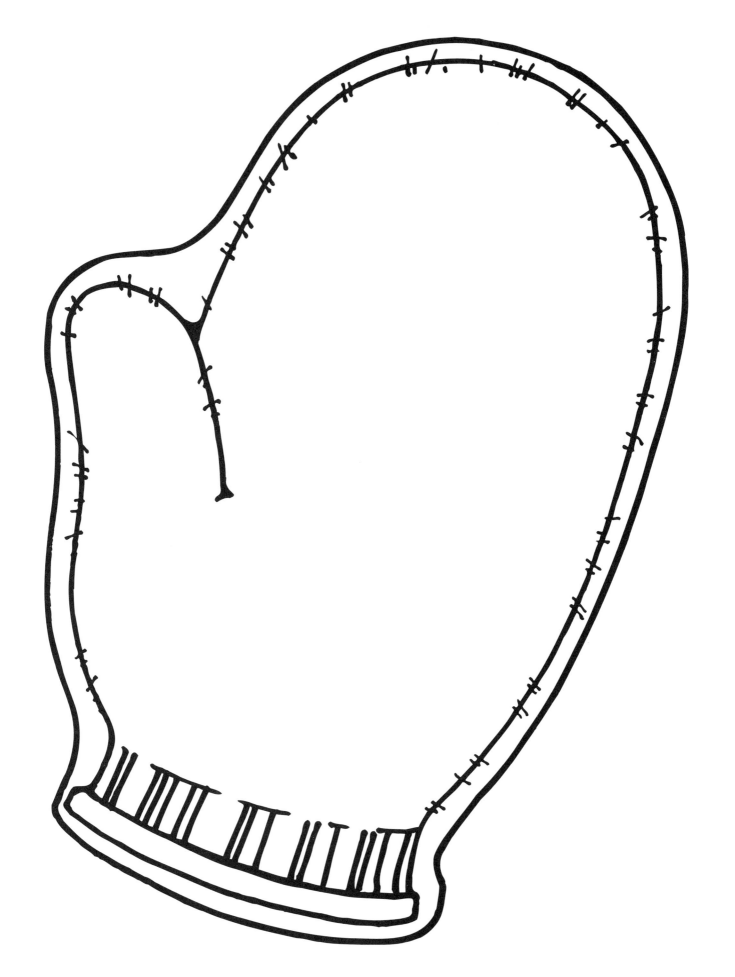

Elvis Presley's Birthday

January 8

Setting the Stage

- Display Elvis paraphernalia and records to gather interest in this day.

- Dress like Elvis in a white T-shirt with rolled-up sleeves, dark pants, black jacket and pompadour hair. Don't forget to curl your lip in true Elvis style!

- Display old records (or make your own from black construction paper) on a bulletin board. Add the caption: "Top 10 Hits!" When students write book reports on record labels (page 57), they can be added to the board.

Historical Background

This American Rock and Roll legend was born on this day in 1935.

Literary Exploration

Elvis Presley by Vanora Leigh
Elvis Presley: The King by Katherine Krohn
"Rock and Roll Band" poem from *A Light in the Attic* by Shel Silverstein

Language Experience

• Let students write book reports on record (LP) patterns to be used in a bulletin board display (see page 56). (Example: "Introducing the new hit, 'Ira Sleeps Over,' performed by the one and only Bernard Waber!") See reproducible on page 60.

Writing Experience

• Students will enjoy writing new lyrics to an Elvis tune. (Example: "Ain't nothin' but a reader . . . all the day long!)

Science/Health Experience

• Discuss when the Earth does its own type of "Rock and Roll" (earthquakes). What conditions cause such movements?

Social Studies Experience

• Study the history of rock and roll music which hit it big with the song "Rock Around the Clock" in 1954. Study some big names, such as the Beatles. Chart them and other rock and rollers on a time line.

Music/Dramatic Experience

• Check out some of Elvis' music from a local library and play it for your class. Some students will enjoy grabbing a ruler (for a microphone) and trying to lip-sync the music.

• Play musical chairs to some of Elvis' music!

Physical/Sensory Experience

• Teach some 50s and 60s dance moves such as the "Twist" to your students.

Arts/Crafts Experience

• Tell students that Elvis' home was called "Graceland." Ask them to imagine what Graceland looks like and work together on a class mural of it.

• Have students trace a guitar pattern to make their own individual guitars (that they can "play" to Elvis' music). The guitars can be painted and details made with dark markers. Even glitter can be added! See reproducibles on pages 61-62.

Extension Activities

• Invite local talent (Elvis-wannabes) to share their talents with your class.

⚠ Serve "Presley's Pretzels" as an afternoon snack!

Values Education Experience

• Explain the tragedy of Elvis' final days because of personal addictions. Talk about how some talented people's careers are cut short because of abuses with alcohol or drugs. How can we avoid these mistakes?

Follow-Up/Homework Idea

• Ask each student to make up a song with his or her name in it. Encourage them to check out an Elvis movie to watch with their families.

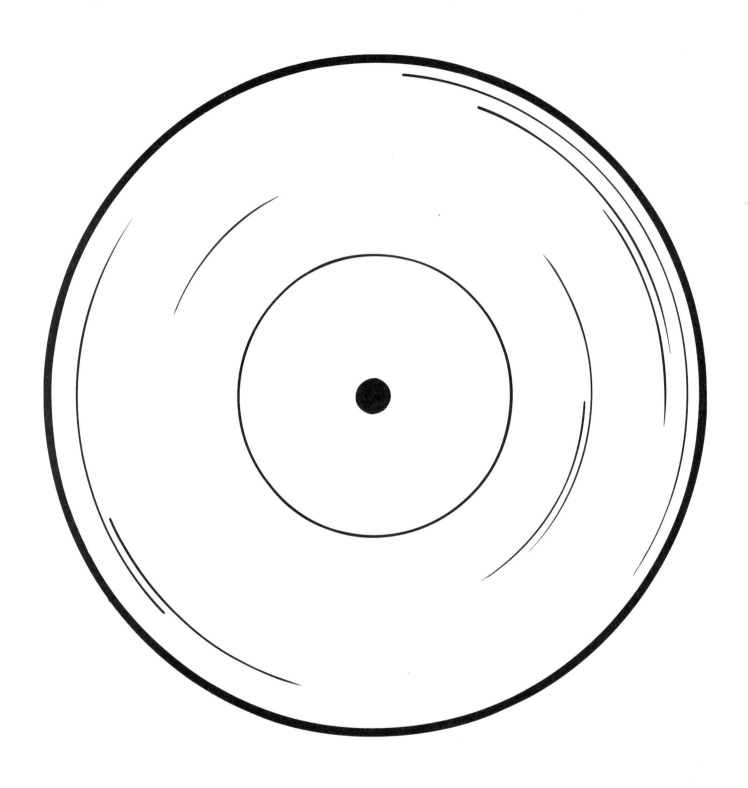

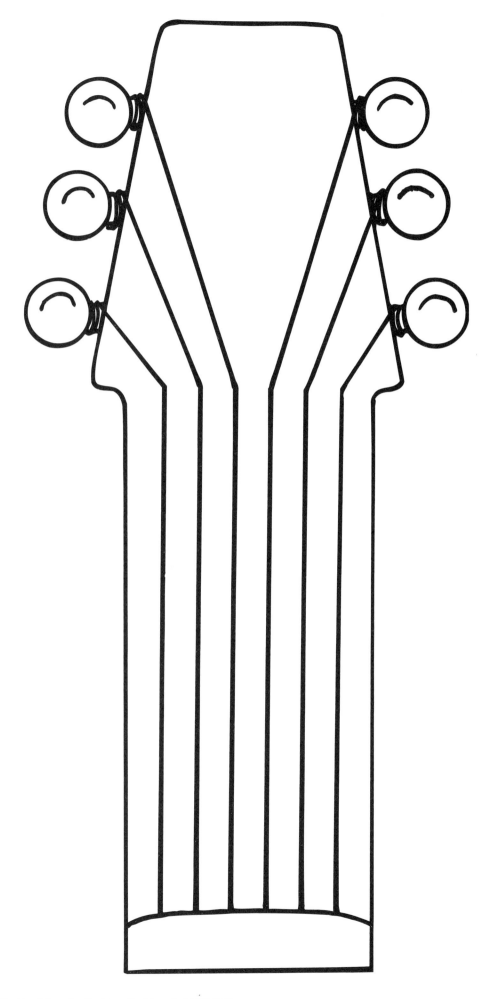

62

Richard Nixon's Birthday

January 9

Historical Background

Richard Milhous Nixon was the 37th President of the United States. He was born on this day in 1913.

Literary Exploration

The Importance of Richard M. Nixon by Roger Barr
The Picture Life of Richard Milhous Nixon by Ann Campbell
Richard M. Nixon, President by L. Edmond Leipold
Richard M. Nixon, President by Sallie Randolph
Richard M. Nixon: The Thirty-Seventh President by Jim Hargrove
Richard M. Nixon: 37th President of the United States by Rebecca Stefoff
Richard Nixon by Dee Lillegard
Richard Nixon: Rise and Fall of a President by Rebecca Larsen

Social Studies Experience

• Study President Nixon's presidency.

Music/Dramatic Experience

• Divide into groups and let students debate the responsibility of role models.

Extension Activities

• Invite a school student leader to come to your class and discuss the importance of honest and exemplary leadership.

• In 1972, President Nixon made an historic visit to China which ended decades of silence between the two countries. A famous photograph shows President and Mrs. Nixon at the Great Wall of China. Research this amazing structure with your students. Did they know that the Great Wall is the only man-made structure on the surface of the Earth which is visible from outer space?

Values Education Experience

• Although Nixon resigned before facing certain impeachment, he suffered the loss of his good name and his achievements as President became overshadowed by the Watergate scandal for the rest of his days. This might be a good time to reflect upon the idea of justice and mercy and its role in our present system of government.

TLC10466 Copyright © Teaching & Learning Company, Carthage, IL 62321-0010

Let It Snow Day

January 10

Setting the Stage

- Display student work or art with the caption: "Winter Wonderland!" Add a snowman and "wintry" decorations. Students can draw pictures of people skiing and glue craft stick skis on them. Let them stuff white plastic garbage bags with newspaper or cotton batting and decorate them with markers and winter clothes to make snowmen for class mascots! Hang leftover Christmas tree "icicles" all around the board.

- Display book jackets with pictures of students bundled up in winter clothes and the caption: "Warm up with a Good Book!"

- Set up an activity center for indoor, bad-weather days with the caption: "Winter Warm-Ups." Include suggestions or activities that can be done during indoor recess or for fast finishers.

- Construct a semantic map or web around the word *snow*. Let students map out all they know or understand about it. Then ask them to list what they would like to learn about snow during the course of the day.

Literary Exploration

The Big Snow by Berta and Elmer Hader
Destination, Antarctica by Robert Swan
First Snow by Kim Lewis
First Snow by Emily Arnold McCully
Geraldine's Big Snow by Holly Keller
Hello, Snow! by Wendy Cheyette Lewison
Katy and the Big Snow by Virginia Lee Burton
Look! Snow! by Kathryn Galbraith
Oh Snow by Monica Mayper
Our Snowman by M. B. Goffstein
The Snow by John Burningham
Snow by Isao Sasaki
Snow by Kathleen Todd
The Snow Angel by Angela McAllister
Snow Babies by Eric Rosser
Snow Crystals by W. A. Bentley
Snow Day by Betsy Maestro
Snow Is Falling by Franklyn M. Branley
Snow Magic by Harriet Ziefert
Snow: Learning for the Fun of It by John Bianchi
The Snow Lion by David McPhail
The Snow Parade by Barbara Brenner
The Snowman by Raymond Briggs
Snowtime by David Saunders
The Snowy Day by Ezra Jack Keats
Stopping by Woods on a Snowy Evening by Robert Frost
A Walk in the Snow by Phyllis S. Busch
When Will It Snow? by Sydney Hoff
White Snow, Blue Feather by Julie Downing
White Snow, Bright Snow by Alvin Tresselt
The Winter Bear by Ruth Craft and Erik Blegvad

Language Experience

• Brainstorm together what can be done in the snow (create castles and forts, make snow "angels," make tracks, etc.). Or ask students to think of words that rhyme with the word *snow*.

• Let students brainstorm everything they can think of that is cold.

Writing Experience

- Pretend you are getting a new student in your class who has never seen snow. Have students write directions for him on the correct way to make a snowman.

- Brainstorm sensory-imagery words about snow (slushy, icy, melting, freezing, sparkling).

- Imagine that one day it snowed kittens or candy. Have students write about their thoughts and actions on such a day. Or use this story starter: You wake up one day and find it has snowed so hard that . . . See reproducible on page 76.

- Let students write about what a snowman might think as the sun starts to shine on him. See reproducible on page 77.

- Take students outside if there is snow and have them explore their surroundings. Have them write about what they see, hear, smell and can feel.

- Have students write about their favorite things to do in snow.

- Let students use their imaginations to write about the coldest day of the year (when ice cubes came out of the faucet).

Name:

Math Experience

- Students love Snowman Math! Give each student a snowman head and white circles or use the patterns on page 78. Have each student write a number on each circle or snowman part for a math problem. Have students form small groups and put together their snowman math problems.

- Let students estimate the number of "snowballs" (mini marshmallows) in a clear jar.

- Write numbers on the board leaving spaces in between. Allow students time to cut large snowballs from white construction paper. Students write problems on the snowballs to match the answers on the board. (Examples: 16 on the board matches snowball problems such as 10 + 6, 18 - 2, 2 x 8 or 4 x 4.) Make a game out of it by mixing up snowballs, then having students pick snowballs to place under the right answer.

Math Experience continued

• Put a snowball in a glass jar and let students predict what will happen to it indoors. Let them estimate how full the jar will be with liquid by the time it completely melts. Let students mark on the jar to track it throughout the day. How close will the students' predictions be to the final liquid level?

HEIDI →

JOHN →

KAYLA →

Science/Health Experience

• Learn about the science of snowflakes! During a snowstorm let students have a first-hand look at the fragile crystals through a magnifying glass.

• Check the snow for tracks made by people, birds or animals.

• Keep track of how much snow falls in your schoolyard by placing a ruler in a tub. Each day, make a mark on the ruler to show the depth of the snow. Compare the measurements with those of the local weather station. Let students make predictions of the amount of snow you'll collect by the end of the month or winter season.

Science/Health Experience continued

- Discuss winter safety! Many accidents can be avoided by knowing the dangers of icy walkways and sledding or skating. Let students suggest some safety rules.

Social Studies Experience

- Locate or identify areas of the world where snow is common. Where do these areas lie on a world map?

Music/Dramatic Experience

- Sing the Christmas favorites, "Let It Snow, Let It Snow, Let It Snow" and "Frosty, the Snowman."

- Students can pretend to be melting snowmen to the familiar tune, "Once There Was a Snowman."

- Play music appropriate to the season: "Dance of the Sugar Plum Fairy" by Tchaikovsky, Debussey's "Snow Is Dancing" or "Footprints in the Snow" (Prelude #6), or Prokofiev's "Waltz on the Ice."

Physical/Sensory Experience

• Play Freeze Tag! One person is "It" and tags another who becomes "frozen." That person stays frozen until another student crawls through his or her legs. Then the "frozen" one "melts."

• Play Pin the Carrot Nose on the Snowman (a variation of Pin the Tail on the Donkey). Trace the snowman on page 77 (without his nose). Cut a carrot nose from orange paper.

• If there is snow outside, build a big snowman or make snow "angels!"

• Get involved in a neighborhood service project shoveling walkways for older neighbors near your school.

Arts/Crafts Experience

• Make "meltless" snowflakes by folding and cutting paper. Fold a square piece of paper once into a triangle. (2) Fold in half to form a smaller triangle, then in half again. (3) Fold in half again to form a cone shape. (4) Cut triangles or interesting shapes into each side of the cone. (5) Then unfold it! Hang them all around the room for a "wintry" feel even if it doesn't snow where you live.

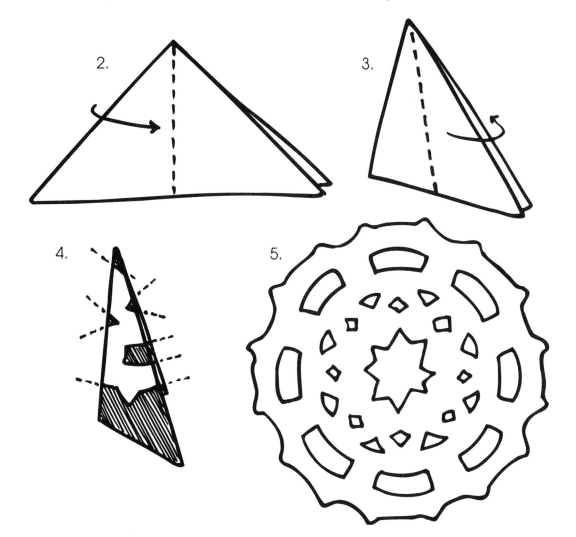

Arts/Crafts Experience continued

- If there is no snow today, students can make "snowmen" out of modeling clay.

- Adapt snow fun to your own climate with artificial snow made of shaving cream or whipped Ivory Snowflakes™. Ivory Snowflakes™ can be whipped with a beater (two parts Ivory Snowflakes™ to one part water) for students to feel and mold! It can be dried overnight on wax paper.

- Build snow sculptures from sugar cubes or miniature marshmallows!

- Students can make beautiful snow scenes (incorporating positive and negative space) by sketching and cutting out a simple picture on a paper plate. When the plate is mounted on a sheet of black construction paper, it's a beautiful silhouette.

- Let students create "snow-like" pictures by gluing cotton balls, batting, torn white paper or foam packaging to dark blue construction paper pictures. White tempera paint or chalk against a dark blue or black background also makes a beautiful effect.

- Make snow scenes in baby food jars. Have students use steel wool to remove the wax coating from the lid. Let them glue small plastic figures to the inside of the lid with waterproof glue. While it is drying, they can fill the jar with water and add $1^1/_2$ teaspoon. of minute tapioca. Let it sit for a couple of days to soak. Then pour the mixture through a fine strainer. Students fill the jars with fresh water, replace the strained tapioca and glue on the lid with waterproof glue or silicone sealer. Let it dry. Then when students shake the jars, they'll see a "snowstorm" scene.

- Here's an easy and fun art activity. Have students draw pictures of snow-time fun with white crayons on white paper. Then they paint over the pictures with blue paint, revealing the picture. They can sprinkle glitter on it before it dries. These pictures create a "wintry feel" in any classroom no matter what the climate.

Arts/Crafts Experience continued

- Students can spray canned "snow" onto dark construction paper, then etch a simple design with a paintbrush handle.

- Spaghetti snowflake art can be made by dipping cooled, cooked, cut spaghetti noodles into a plate of white glue, then arranging them in a snowflake pattern on wax paper. Sprinkle silver glitter on it and let it dry overnight. Suspend from the ceiling with fish line or dental floss for a dazzling effect!

- Have students glue cotton swabs on dark construction paper in snowflake patterns.

Extension Activities

- Find out if there are ice sculpture displays or winter carnivals in your area that your class might visit.

- Weather permitting, have a snow sculpture activity outside! Encourage students to create people, animals or buildings. Divide them into groups and give awards out for the most impressive snow sculptures. Then go inside for hot chocolate and marshmallows to warm up! See award patterns on page 79.

⚠ Make Snow Ice Cream! Mix fresh, clean snow, an egg, 1 tsp. of vanilla and 1/2 cup of sugar (to taste) with 2 cups of milk to the desired consistency. Eat right away! If there is no snow available, crush ice cubes in a blender.

Let It Snow

Let It Snow

Let It Snow

Let It Snow

Extension Activities continued

⚠ Snowman Cupcakes are a snap! Add a white snowball-shaped cupcake on top of another one and make a face with candy corn, gumdrops and chocolate chips.

⚠ A "snow" ice cream soda can be made by mixing a scoop of vanilla ice cream, $1/2$ cup of milk, 1 teaspoon of honey and a drop of food coloring in a blender. Pour into tall cups and fill with fresh, fallen snow.

⚠ Give students three large marshmallows, some toothpicks and raisins or chocolate chips to make snowmen. Provide white icing, a graham cracker and two peppermint sticks to form a "sled" for the snowman to ride.

⚠ Make edible snowflakes. Give each student a flour tortilla to fold in half and gently "tear" into a snowflake design. Unfold it to see the design, then lightly fry the tortilla on both sides. Students can sprinkle a little powdered sugar on top for a "snowy" effect.

⚠ Let each student stick two large marshmallows together with a toothpick, then dip another toothpick in food coloring and draw facial features and buttons on the snowman. When the snowman is ready, float it on top of a mug of hot chocolate!

Extension Activities

⚠ Edible snowflakes can be made by giving students a large marshmallow, 18 toothpicks and 18 miniature marshmallows. The students stick the toothpicks in the large marshmallow, then stick miniature marshmallows to the ends of the toothpicks. They'll end up with yummy snowflakes!

Follow-Up/Homework Idea

• Encourage students to look for things outside that are unique to winter and make observational drawings of them.

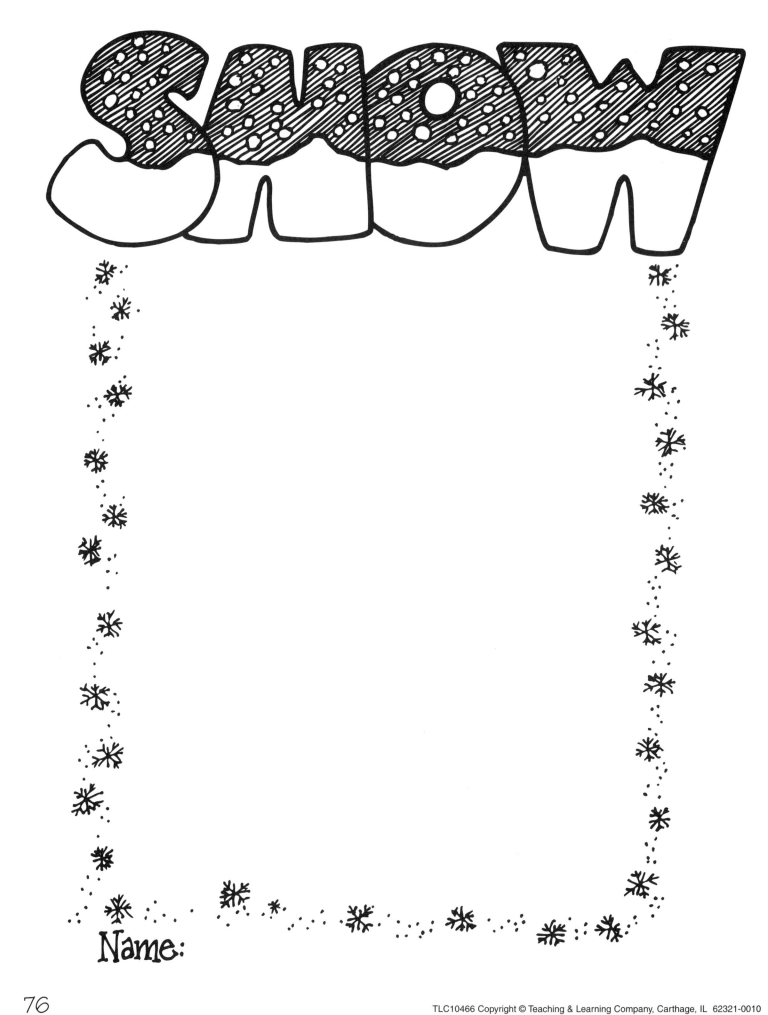

Name:

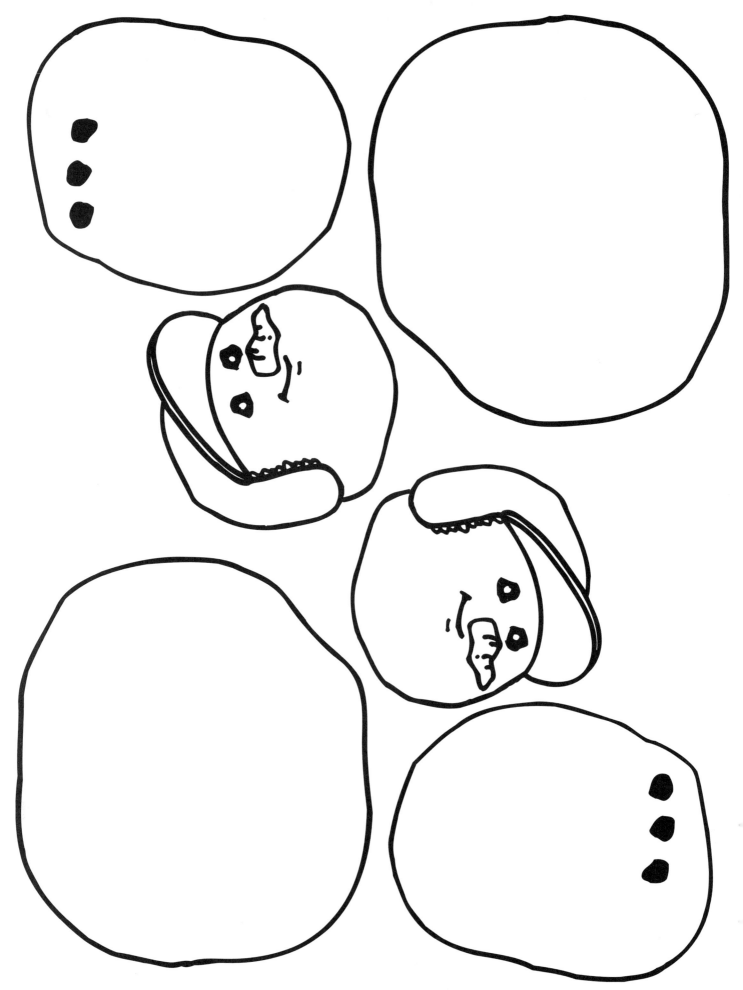

Solo Day

January 11

Setting the Stage

- Today the emphasis will be on students doing things alone. If the desks are normally set up in groups, set them apart just for today.

- Construct a semantic web with words that come to students' minds when they hear the word *alone*.

Historical Background

On this day in 1935, Amelia Earhart was the first woman to fly solo across the Pacific Ocean.

Literary Exploration

The First Solo Flight Around the World by Richard Taylor
The First Solo Transatlantic Flight by Richard L. Taylor
Going Solo by Roald Dahl
Maud Flies Solo by Gibbs Davis
Solo by Kathryn Lasky
Solo Plus One by Ragnhild Scamell

Language Experience

• Jerrie Mock was the first woman to fly solo around the world in 1964. Invite students to share how they felt when they did something for the first time.

Writing Experience

• Ask students to write about their feelings when they are alone. Do they ever feel lonesome? Do they ever feel like they just want to get away by themselves with no one else around? Let them write their thoughts, then invite volunteers to share their feelings with the class. See reproducible on page 84.

Solo
Day

Solo
Day

Solo
Day

Math Experience

• Give students the opportunity to survey others about the kinds of things they like to do alone (read, write poetry, take walks). Let them tally the results and add the information to a class graph.

Social Studies Experience

• Study events surrounding Amelia Earhart's 1935 flight across the Pacific Ocean. Find out what led to her decision to make the flight.

Music/Dramatic Experience

• Invite students to sing solos.

• Encourage interested students to role-play Earhart's triumphant arrival at her final destination in 1935.

Arts/Crafts Experience

• Explain what a hermit is. Challenge students to build or draw a cave or solitary shack in which a hermit might live.

Extension Activities

• Encourage students to visit those who might be feeling alone or lonely (hospital patients or the elderly in a senior citizens home). If possible, schedule a class trip. Brainstorm ways your class could help the people feel less lonely.

Values Education Experience

• Henry David Thoreau lived alone at Walden Pond for a little over two years thinking, observing nature and writing down his ideas. Discuss the merits and value of spending time alone to relax, create or be alone with your own thoughts.

Follow-Up/Homework Idea

• Amelia Earhart loved to read books (especially adventure books). Invite students to read this evening all by themselves.

When I'm alone...

Little Red Riding Hood Day

January 12

Setting the Stage

- Dress up as one of the characters in Charles Perrault's famous stories. (See a partial list below.)

- Display Perrault's books and items that have significance in his books (such as a basket to take to Grandmother's house).

Historical Background

Charles Perrault was a French writer who was born on this day in 1628. He is best known for his collection of folktales such as: "Cinderella," "Puss in Boots," "Sleeping Beauty" and "Little Red Riding Hood."

Literary Exploration

Cinderella by Marcia Brown
Cinderella by Barbara Karlin
Cinderella and Other Tales from Perrault by Charles Perrault
The Complete Fairy Tales of Charles Perrault by Charles Perrault, et al
The Good Witch: A Charles Perrault Tale Retold by Mary Lewis Wang, et al
Little Red Riding Hood by Armand Eisen
Little Red Riding Hood by Paul Galdone
Little Red Riding Hood by Brothers Grimm, et al
Little Red Riding Hood by Trina Schart Hyman
Little Red Riding Hood: A Classic Tale by Eduard Jose, et al
Little Red Riding Hood by Mabel Watts
Lon Pop Po: A Red-Riding Hood Story from China by Ed Young
Moss Gown by William Hooks
Prince Cinders by Babette Cole
Puss in Boots: Based on the Classic Fairy Tale by Charles Perrault by Kurt Baumann, et al
Red Riding Hood by Beatrice de Regniers
Red Riding Hood by James Marshall
Rindercella by Archie Campbell
The Fairy Tales of Charles Perrault by Charles Perrault

Language Experience

• After reading one of Perrault's stories, ask students to fold a sheet of paper into four sections. Have them write and illustrate the four major events of the story in sequential order.

Writing Experience

• Let students change the ending of one of Perrault's familiar stories and share the new version with the class.

• Have each student write a letter from one character to another in one of Perrault's books. (Example: A stepsister writes to Prince Charming about why the shoe didn't fit and why he should choose her instead.)

Social Studies Experience

- Many cultures have their own versions of the fairy tale, Cinderella. Read some of them together. Discuss the differences.
  Abadeha: The Philippine Cinderella by Myrna de la Paz
  Mufaro's Beautiful Daughters by John Steptoe
  Tattercoats by Margaret Greaves
  The Brocaded Slippers and Other Vietnamese Tales by Lynette Vuong
  The Egyptian Cinderella by Shirley Climo
  The Rough-Face Girl by Rafe Martin
  Vasilissa the Beautiful: A Russian Folktale by Elizabeth Winthrop
  Yeh Shen: A Cinderella Story from China by Ai-Ling Louie

- Review some stories Perrault wrote, looking for situations that may be considered unsafe today (such as talking to strangers as Little Red Riding Hood did with the wolf).

Music/Dramatic Experience

- Divide students into small groups and let them act out scenes from Perrault's stories.

- Sing "The Red-Riding Hood Song" by Carmino Ravosa.

Arts/Crafts Experience

- Students can illustrate Perrault's stories on a giant mural or draw and cut out characters, then glue them on craft sticks to make puppets.

Follow-Up/Homework Idea

- Encourage students to go to the library and pick up one of Perrault's fairy tales to read this evening.

Popcorn Day

January 13

Setting the Stage

- Display favorite book jackets coming out of a popcorn container with the caption: "'Pop'ular Books." Add the message: "We're not trying to 'butter' you up but 'pop' on over to the reading area to snack on a good book!" Let students write comments about the books on fluffy popcorn shapes and place them around the book jackets. See patterns on page 97.

- Construct a semantic map or web with information students know about popcorn, then ask them to list questions they want answered as the day progresses.

- Explain that you will drop an unpopped popcorn kernel in a jar each time you see an act of kindness or students staying on task. Pop up the results for the class to enjoy!

TLC10466 Copyright © Teaching & Learning Company, Carthage, IL 62321-0010

Historical Background

Popcorn has been around for a long time. Explorers found popcorn in a cave that was over 5000 years old. Archaeologists found paintings of popcorn that are believed to have been part of Aztec religious ceremonies over 8000 years ago. Popcorn is the oldest of the three main types of corn: field corn, sweet corn and popcorn. Native Americans introduced Pilgrims to popcorn when they came to this country. They liked it so much they served it for breakfast with cream and sugar on it.

Literary Exploration

Corn Is Maize: The Gift of the Indians by Aliki
Cornzapoppin'! by Barbara Williams
I Love Popcorn by Carolyn Vosburg Hall
Mr. Picklepaw's Popcorn by Ruth Joyce Adams
Popcorn by Frank Asch
Popcorn by Millicent Ellis Selsam
The Popcorn Book by Tomie dePaola
Popcorn Days and Buttermilk Nights by Gary Paulsen
The Popcorn Dragon by Jane Thayer
Popcorn Magic by Phyllis Adams
Popcorn Pop? by Jack Myers
The Popcorn Popper by JoAnne Nelson
Princess Rosetta and the Popcorn Man by Mary E. Wilkins
Science Fun with Peanuts and Popcorn by Rose Wyler
Sing a Song of Popcorn by Marcia Brown
Stella and Roy by Ashley Wolff
What Makes Popcorn Pop? by Jack Myers

Language Experience

• How many new words can students make using the letters in *popcorn*?

• During oral reading with your class, warn students that you're going to play "Popcorn." One student reads while others follow along. You tap a shoulder and say "Popcorn." That student picks up reading where the other person left off or is asked a question about what was just read. It keeps students on their toes and increases comprehension awareness.

• Hand out popped and unpopped popcorn to reinforce skills with "Popcorn Punctuation!" Have each student write a paragraph (in larger penmanship than usual) using popped popcorn for periods and popcorn kernels for commas and quotation marks. Exclamation marks can be made with a kernel and a piece of popped corn.

Writing Experience

• Have students write about what would happen if popcorn exploded after it was eaten.

• Let students use their imagination to write what happens when they open the door and find the classroom filled to the ceiling with popcorn!

• Brainstorm together sensory imagery words to describe popcorn.

• Students can ask questions about popcorn or send for popcorn materials by writing to:

The Popcorn Institute
401 N. Michigan Ave.
Chicago, IL 60611-4267

• See reproducible for "Writing Experience" on page 98.

Math Experience

• When popcorn is popped, it puffs up about 30 times its original size. Let students estimate and make drawings of how other familiar objects might look at 30 times their original size.

• Compare various sizes and colors of corn (popcorn, Indian corn, field corn and dried corn). Compare them on a class graph.

• Make some popcorn bags and write a number on the front of each with dark marker. Let students write math problems on popcorn shapes to go in the bags. (Examples, a bag with a 12 on it could have these popcorn shapes: 6 + 6, 15 - 3, 3 x 4.) Mix up the popcorn shapes and have students match them with the right bags. See pattern for popcorn shapes on page 97 and pattern for popcorn bag on page 99.

Popcorn

Popcorn

Popcorn

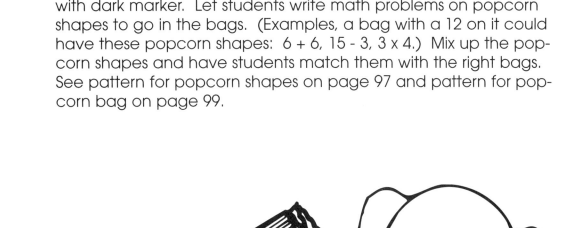

Math Experience

- Let students estimate how many popcorn kernels are in a jar.

- Use popcorn kernels as counters or manipulatives in math today!

- To play this math game, one student crouches behind another student's desk. The teacher or student leader gives a math problem. The one who can answer it first "pops" up and gives the answer. Whoever answers correctly, gets to sit in the desk. Continue the game around the class.

- Get the class involved in whole-class estimating by displaying different sizes of bowls. Have students estimate how many popped kernels will fill up each bowl.

- Younger students can glue the correct number of popcorn pieces next to numbers on heavy construction paper. Tracing over the numbers with a finger provides a great tactile experience for early learners.

⚠ Have each student grab a handful of popcorn, estimate the number of pieces and record the number. Then they can count to find the actual amount and record it before eating the popcorn. Check to see if their estimations get closer with practice.

Science/Health Experience

- Read *What Makes Popcorn Pop?* by Jack Myers. Popcorn contains water which, when heated turns to steam. Trapped within the kernel, the steam pushes outward and explodes. Heat some Jiffy Pop Popcorn™ on a hot burner so students can watch the popcorn puff up and expand before their very eyes!

Popcorn

- Popcorn can be a nutritious treat that is low in sugar and calories and high in carbohydrates. Explore other nutritious possibilities for quick and easy snacks.

- Let students sprout popcorn kernels. Provide zip-type sandwich bags and popcorn kernels. After they spoon a little potting soil into the bag, they add a little water and bury the kernels about an inch deep. After the bags are sealed and displayed in a sunny area, students can watch over the next few days to see when the kernels begin to sprout.

Popcorn

- Browse through *Science Fun with Peanuts and Popcorn* by Rose Wyler for some fun science experiments!

Popcorn

Social Studies Experience

• Throughout history, corn has been cooked in many ways. Native Americans used to pop an ear of corn by putting it on a stick and holding it over a fire, throwing kernels right into the fire by the handfuls or filling clay pots with hot sand, then throwing popcorn in and stirring with a stick. Legend has it that Quadequina (Chief Massasoit's brother) brought bushels of popcorn to share at the first Thanksgiving feast. Ask students if they were to bring a bushel of something to share, what would it be?

Music/Dramatic Experience

• Sing "Popcorn Popping" (by Georgia W. Bella and Betty Lou Cooney). Students can act out or use hand signals for each part.

• Imagine that the popcorn industry is feeling a drop in sales. Let students form groups and write jingles or perform commercials to encourage popcorn sales.

Physical/Sensory Experience

• Pop popcorn over a clean plastic tablecloth so students can watch it pop all over the place. Let students examine the kernels, noting the tough outer coat of each seed. Explain that the kernels contain baby plants and stored food that contains starch and water. Show them that corn kernels (from an ear of corn) are dried to make popcorn. As a transition activity before going out for recess, let each student curl into a ball and "burst" like a popcorn kernel.

Popcorn

Popcorn

Popcorn

Arts/Crafts Experience

- After singing about "Popcorn popping on the apricot tree," the students can make popcorn "blossoms" on a tree. They dab a small amount of brown paint on paper, then blow through a straw to move the paint upwards towards the top of the paper (making a trunk and then branches). They can glue popped popcorn "blossoms" to the tree branches.

- Give each student a popcorn kernel to examine from all angles. Have them draw the shape on a sheet of paper, then create something out of it. Let them give it a title and write about it at the bottom of the sheet before sharing the creation with the class.

- String popcorn and place it around branches outside for birds to eat!

- Native Americans introduced popcorn to the Pilgrims as food, but also wore it as jewelry. Let students make bracelets or necklaces from popcorn. Provide blunt needles and dental floss for the students to thread the popcorn. Large paper clips could also be bent and used as needles.

- Let students make Indian mosaic pictures from popcorn kernels dipped in dry tempera paint and glued on heavy construction paper.

Extension Activities

⚠ Have a popcorn party! Pop lots of popcorn (or make varieties such as cheese or caramel flavored). Serve it with punch or juice. Let students munch while other students lip-sync a favorite song.

⚠ Try eating popcorn like the Pilgrims did, with cream and sugar, or make popcorn soup by serving tomato soup with popcorn in it!

⚠ Make these yummy popcorn balls!

Popcorn

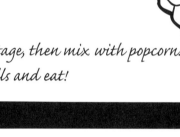

Popcorn Balls

Pop about 6 cups of popcorn.

Boil this mixture:

1 c. sugar

3/4 c. water

3 T. light corn syrup

Dash of salt

1/2 t. vinegar

Boil to a hard crack stage, then mix with popcorn.

Form into popcorn balls and eat!

Popcorn

Follow-Up/Homework Idea

• Students can pop some popcorn and share the tasty treat with their families.

Popcorn

Glue here

HOT TASTY POPCORN

Fan fold ⤴

Fold up bottom and staple.

Fan fold ⤴

African Safari Day

January 14

Setting the Stage

- Construct a semantic map or web with facts students know (or would like to know) about Africa.

Historical Background

The great humanitarian, Albert Schweitzer, was born on this day in 1875. Schweitzer was a German physician and musician who could have lived his life in luxury, but chose instead to go to Africa to work as a missionary bringing medicine and a hospital to the poor.

Literary Exploration

Albert Schweitzer by James Bentley
Albert Schweitzer by Gabriella Cremaschi
Albert Schweitzer by Kenneth G. Richards
Albert Schweitzer: Genius in the Jungle by Joseph Gollomb
Story of Albert Schweitzer by Jo Manton
The Value of Dedication: The Story of Albert Schweitzer by Spencer Johnson

Language Experience

• Try Albert's African Alphabetizing. Brainstorm animals that might live in Africa, then let students put them in alphabetical order.

Writing Experience

• Ask students to write about when someone helped them and really made a difference.

• Students can write about how they would like to help solve specific world problems as Schweitzer did. See reproducible on page 105.

I can make a difference...

Science/Health Experience

• Discuss the primitive health conditions of some parts of Africa and how easily disease could be spread.

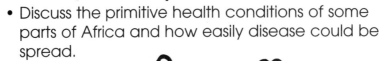

Social Studies Experience

• Research Albert Schweitzer's great humanitarian contributions.

Music/Dramatic Experience

• Give students scenarios where service opportunities present themselves. (Examples: a student carrying a lot of books tries to open a door, or a student cannot find the glue he needs for a project.) Encourage students to look out for the needs of those around them and to respond accordingly.

Arts/Crafts Experience

- Students can create service coupon books with coupons good for helping others (such as helping the custodian with playground cleanup or helping the librarian shelve books). See reproducibles on page 106.

- Have students paint a large mural of a world in which people are involved in countless acts of kindness and service.

Extension Activities

- Begin a daily tradition of having a Secret Service Agent in your classroom. Each morning select a different person to look for and carry out small acts of service (such as holding doors open for others) throughout the day. Reinforce the idea that he or she is a "Secret" Service Agent. If students help others for recognition, it becomes self-serving and deflects from the original purpose of serving.

- Let students make gifts to take to an orphanage or to shut-ins.

African
Safari

African
Safari

African
Safari

Values Education Experience

• Discuss how serving others makes you feel inside.

• When Albert Schweitzer was about eight years old he was with a friend, aiming his slingshot at birds. Albert had mixed feelings: he didn't want to hurt the birds, but was afraid his friend would laugh at him if he said so. As he was taking aim at a bird, he heard church bells ringing in the distance. The bells had a great impact on him. He threw the slingshot down and ran home. From then on, he worried less about what others thought of him and more about being true to himself. Discuss with students how to be true to themselves in the face of peer pressure and not let others lead them into doing what they feel is not right. Talk about the importance of listening to and following their own hearts.

Follow-Up/Homework Idea

• Encourage students to do acts of anonymous service for family members.

I can make a difference...

I Care Coupon

To: _____

Good for one: _____

From: _____

I Care Coupon

To: _____

Good for one: _____

From: _____

I Care Coupon

To: _____

Good for one: _____

From: _____

Martin Luther King, Jr.'s Birthday

January 15

Setting the Stage

- Have students trace their hands on red, white or blue construction paper and cut them out. At the top of a bulletin board, mount the caption: "Joining Hands for . . ." Arrange the red, white and blue hands into the word *peace* underneath.

- Encourage unity with this bulletin board idea! At the top of the board, mount the caption: "We are more alike than different!" Have students draw self-portraits (head and neck). On the shoulders they can write ways people are alike (color, race, nationality, religion, economic circumstances). (Examples: "We all smile in the very same language" or "We all need love.") See reproducible on page 112.

- Construct a semantic map or web with facts students know about Dr. Martin Luther King, Jr. Then let them ask questions they would like answered during the day.

Martin Luther King, Jr.

Martin Luther King, Jr.

Historical Background

Dr. Martin Luther King, Jr. was an influential American civil rights leader born on this day in 1929.

Literary Exploration

About Martin Luther King Day by Mary Virginia Fox
The Day Martin Luther King, Jr., Was Shot by Jim Haskins
Happy Birthday, Martin Luther King by Jean Marzollo
I Have a Dream: The Story of Martin Luther King by Margaret Davidson
. . . If You Lived at the Time of Martin Luther King by Ellen Levine
Let Freedom Ring: A Ballad of Martin Luther King, Jr. by Myra Cohn
    Livingston
The Life and Words of Martin Luther King Jr. by Ira Peck
Marching to Freedom: The Story of Martin Luther King, Jr. by Joyce
    Milton
Martin Luther King by Rosemary Bray
Martin Luther King Day by Janet McDonnell
Martin Luther King, Jr.: A Picture Story by Margaret Boone-Jones
Martin Luther King, Jr.: A Man to Remember by Patricia McKissack
Martin Luther King Jr.: A Man Who Changed Things by Carol Greene
Martin Luther King, Jr. Day by Linda Lowery
Martin Luther King, Jr. Day by Dianne MacMillan
Martin Luther King, Jr.: Free at Last by David A. Adler
Martin Luther King: The Peaceful Warrior by Ed Clayton
A Picture Book of Martin Luther King, Jr. by David A. Adler
Thank You, Dr. Martin Luther King, Jr. by Eleanora E. Tate

Language Experience

• Read excerpts from Dr. King's famous "I Have a Dream" speech, discussing each part with your class and explaining unfamiliar vocabulary.

TLC10466 Copyright © Teaching & Learning Company, Carthage, IL 62321-0010

Writing Experience

- Martin Luther King, Jr. is known for his speech in which he tells about the dream he has for the world he hopes his children will live in. Have students write about their dreams for the kind of world they would like to live in. See reproducible on page 113.

- Abraham Lincoln and George Washington have Presidents' Day named in their honor. Martin Luther King, Jr. has a day named for him. Ask students to write about someone they think should have a holiday named after him or her.

Name:

Social Studies Experience

- Have students research the life of Martin Luther King, Jr. and his efforts to further the cause of civil rights. They can make a time line depicting significant events in his life or important milestones in the civil rights movement.

- Dr. King was known for his ability to bring about changes for good through non-violence. Some students may not have had appropriate modeling for how to handle conflict or bring about change peacefully. Set up a conflict-resolution area in your room with two chairs or two desks in an area by themselves. Post on the wall or desk by this area these cue cards: "What do I think happened? Why do I think it happened? What was my responsibility in it or how could I have prevented it from happening? What do I think should happen now?" This will help students admit their part in the conflict. As need arises, students can go to the area and write or talk quietly about the steps to resolve the conflict (using the cue cards as a springboard for thought or discussion). Introduce the area with role-playing scenarios. Then when the time comes and emotions are high, students will know what to do.

Physical/Sensory Experience

• Martin Luther King, Jr. was known for peaceful civil rights demonstrations and rallies. If you have access to software programs with clips of his famous "I Have a Dream" speech, let students watch them. Stage your own class peace march. Students can make peace-promoting posters, attach them to rulers and carry them around the school.

• Illustrate how we are more alike than different with this object lesson. Ask each student to examine a box of crayons, noting similarities and differences. They will find that all the crayons are made from the same products and chemicals and structurally have the same components. The only difference is the pigment or color of each crayon. People are also made the same (structurally) with the same needs for survival and love. Our outside packages may vary in color of skin but that adds variety and diversity that we can appreciate in one another.

Arts/Crafts Experience

• Martin Luther King, Jr. received the Nobel Peace Prize in 1964. Have students make their own class "Peace Prizes" out of blue satin ribbon. They can cut out the patterns on page 114 and glue it or tie it on a ribbon. Keep some on hand. When students demonstrate peaceful resolutions of difficulties, award the "Peace Prize" from the class.

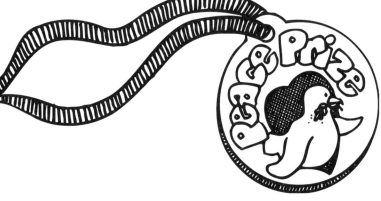

Extension Activities

⚠ Serve cupcakes with doves (symbol of peace) on the top. See dove patterns on page 115.

Extension Activities continued

⚠ Shape refrigerator dough breadsticks into "peace" symbols (a circular shape with an upside-down "Y" in the middle) to eat.

• Try this thought-provoking object lesson on older students. Without telling students, decide on an arbitrary criteria for an experiment (red hair, blue eyes, etc.). Show obvious favoritism to a select group, letting them line up first, etc. It won't be long before someone's sense of justice and fair play will kick in. Resentment may start to build. Those who get special treatment will probably start feeling anxious, too. Take care that feelings are not hurt and that no extremes are involved. The most important thing is for students to see the injustice in prejudice of any kind. Help them understand that we need to work together instead of pitting ourselves against one another. When you feel the timing is appropriate, use this experiment as a lead-in for acceptance of others. Explain that in America some people (such as Native Americans and African Americans) were not given fair treatment for many years (not allowed to vote, sent to schools with less desirable resources, etc.). Discuss the injustice of this kind of treatment.

Martin Luther King, Jr.

Values Education Experience

• Reinforce the value of unity. Point out that this country is called the "United" States of America. What would happen to the nation if we weren't united?

Martin Luther King, Jr.

Follow-Up/Homework Idea

• Challenge students to practice peaceful conflict resolution within their own families.

Martin Luther King, Jr.

"We are more alike than different!"

Name:

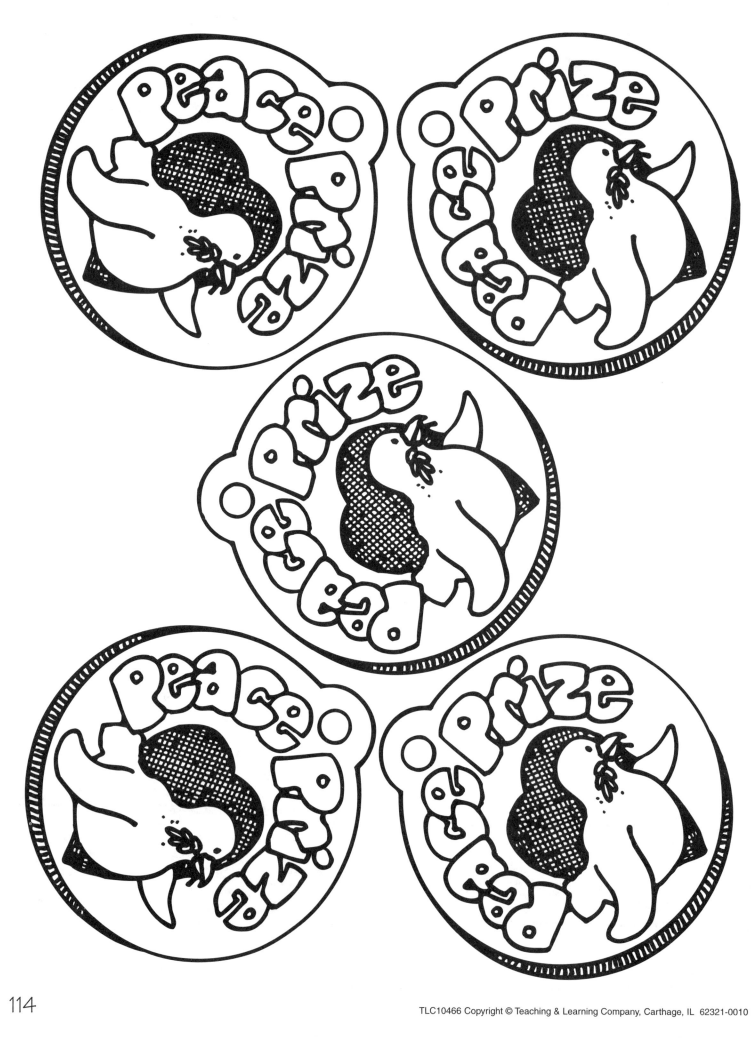

114

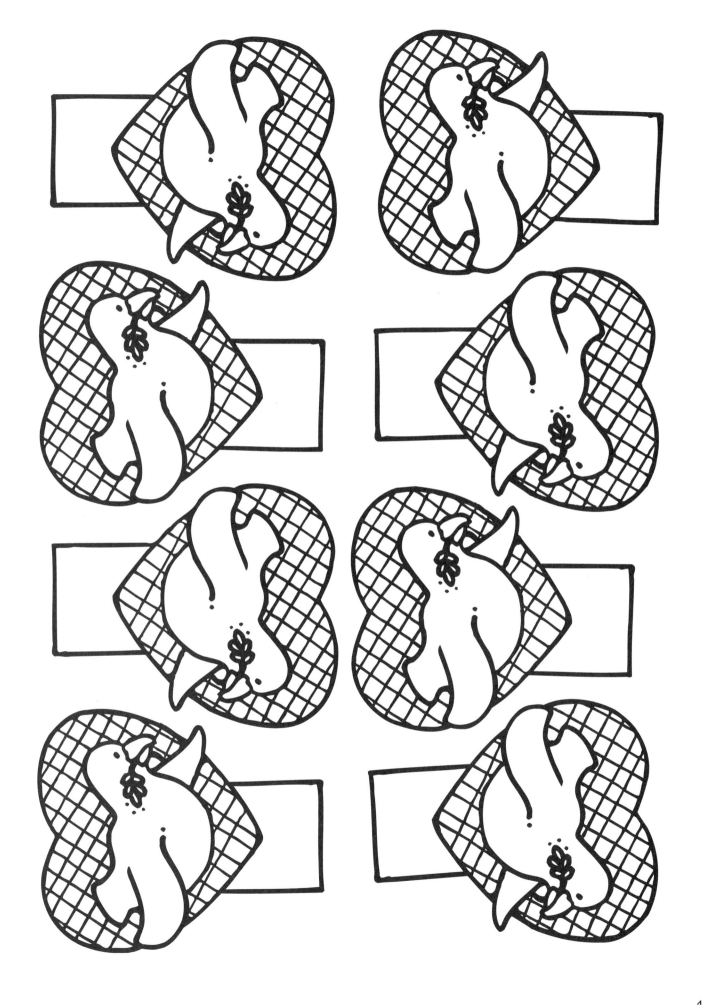

Nothing Day

January 16

Nothing
Day

Setting the Stage

• Pose this question to your students: Do you think children today have more or less to do than children born 100 years ago? Pretend that you know of a terrible disease plaguing children everywhere—boredom. Some students say they have nothing to do after school or during the summer. Should children have full schedules planned by parents to provide never-ending activities and entertainment or should students provide their own pursuits, activities and service opportunities? Let students share their feelings.

Nothing
Day

Historical Background

There's nothing like sitting in the middle of January with the excitement of the holidays over and nothing to do, to start making everyone feel "cabin fever" and restless. This is a silly day set aside to cure boredom and spawn the creativity from within.

Nothing
Day

Literary Exploration

A Bag Full of Nothing by Jay Williams
"Bored" a poem from *Light in the Attic* by Shel Silverstein
Bored, Nothing to Do by Peter Spier
A Box of Nothing by Peter Dickinson
Less Than Nothing Is Really Something by Robert Froman
Nothing at All! by Denys Cazet
Nothing Ever Happens on My Block by Ellen Raskin
Nothing Happened by Bill Harley
Nothing to Do by Liza Alexander
Nothing to Do by Russell Hoban
Nothing-to-Do Puppy by Cindy Szekeres
Superkids: Creative Learning Activities for Kids by Jean Marzollo
There's Nothing to Do! by James Stevenson

Language Experience

• Let students brainstorm ideas of what to do when "there's nothing to do."

Writing Experience

• Have students list activities to do after school when homework is done and there's "nothing to do." The ideas can be set up in sub-categories, such as:

> Things to Do That Are Free
> Things to Do That Are Close to Home
> Things to Do All by Myself
> Things to Do with Another Person
> Things to When It's Rainy Outside
> Things to Do Outdoors

These ideas can be written on Fun-2-Do cards and put in each student's Fun-2-Do box (page 119). See card reproducibles on page 120.

Math Experience

• Let students survey other students about what they like to do when "there's nothing to do." They can tally the results and add them to a class bar graph.

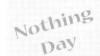

Science/Health Experience

• Let students brainstorm what they would like to know in the fields of science and health so they can begin research in their spare time. (Examples: One student might want to learn more about robotics while another wants to learn why we get colds in the winter.)

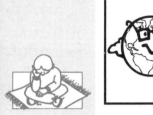

Social Studies Experience

• Have students think of people throughout history they would like to know more about (such as Joan of Arc) or a period of history (such as the Dark Ages). They can begin additional study as they find themselves with "nothing to do."

Music/Dramatic Experience

• Students can make up new words to a familiar tune or spice up an old tired story by acting it out with a few friends.

Physical/Sensory Experience

• Students can brainstorm their favorite indoor and outdoor activities and games (a sure cure for "cabin fever").

Arts/Crafts Experience

- Let students decorate a shoe box or tissue box with felt, fabric, construction paper, rickrack, lace or anything on hand. The container can hold all their creative ideas as they come up with them so that when school is out and summer arrives with "nothing to do," they will have plenty of ideas to choose from. See pattern for the Fun-2-Do box lid and stickers on page 121.

Values Education Experience

- Discuss the value of personal accountability and responsibility. Why do students often prefer to have someone else "take care of things" for them? Why is it important for them to be personally responsible for some things in their lives?

Follow-Up/Homework Idea

- Encourage students to look for ways to fill their time with good, wholesome service opportunities and fun!

FUN · 2 · DO!

FUN · 2 · DO!

FUN · 2 · DO!

FUN · 2 · DO!

FUN · 2 · DO!

FUN · 2 · DO!

FUN · 2 · DO!

FUN · 2 · DO!

FUN · 2 · DO!

FUN · 2 · DO!

Benjamin Franklin's Birthday

January 17

Setting the Stage
- Display a skeleton key next to a kite, a pair of glasses and a copy of *Poor Richard's Almanac*.

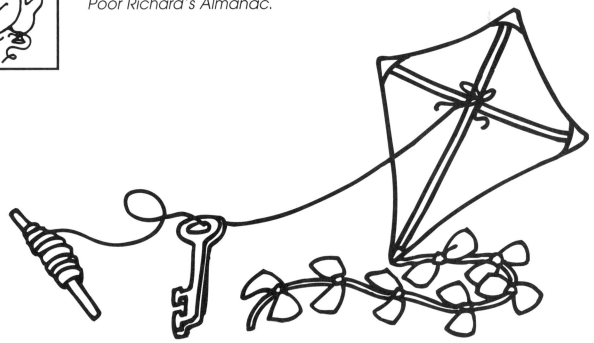

- Construct a semantic map or web with facts your students already know about Benjamin Franklin. Then ask them to write questions they would like answered in today's activities.

Historical Background
Benjamin Franklin was an influential American statesman, philosopher and scientist. He was born on this day in 1706, the youngest son of Josiah and Abiah Franklin's 17 children.

Literary Exploration

Ben and Me by Robert Lawson
Ben Franklin's Glass Armonica by Bryna Stevens
Benjamin Franklin by Ingri D'Aulaire
Benjamin Franklin by Susan Dye Lee
Benjamin Franklin by Chris Looby
Benjamin Franklin by Robert R. Potter
Benjamin Franklin by Cass R. Sandak
Benjamin Franklin by R. Conrad Stein
Benjamin Franklin by Gail B. Stewart
Benjamin Franklin and His Friends by Robert Quackenbush
Benjamin Franklin: A Man with Many Jobs by Carol Greene
Benjamin Franklin: Scientist and Inventor by Eve Feldman
Benjamin Franklin, Young Printer by Augusta Stevenson
The Many Lives of Benjamin Franklin by Aliki
Meet Benjamin Franklin by Maggi Scarf
A Picture Book of Ben Franklin by David A. Adler
The Real Book About Benjamin Franklin by Sam Epstein
The Story of Benjamin Franklin, Amazing American by Margaret Davidson
The Value of Saving: The Story of Benjamin Franklin by Spencer Johnson
What's the Big IDEA, Ben Franklin? by Jean Fritz

Language Experience

• Ben Franklin developed many important inventions during his lifetime. Brainstorm some of these together, then let students put the inventions in alphabetical order.

Writing Experience

• Franklin's *Poor Richard's Almanac* was (in part) a compilation of some of his words of wisdom such as, "Early to bed, early to rise, makes a man healthy, wealthy and wise." Let students compile a classroom almanac with their own words of wisdom that would make Franklin proud!

• Since Benjamin was one of 17 children, he probably had to do his fair share of giving and taking. Ask students to write what it might have been like in the Franklin household.

Science/Health Experience

- Benjamin Franklin gained valuable insight as a result of his experiments with a kite, a key and electricity, but "don't try this at home." Talk about what could have happened to him. Review electrical safety with your class.

Social Studies Experience

- Study the time period when Benjamin Franklin lived, his life and some of his contributions.

Music/Dramatic Experience

- Let students act out some important events in Benjamin Franklin's life.

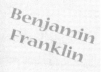

Physical/Sensory Experience

- Blindfold one student at a time and play Pin the Key on the Kite (a version of Pin the Tail on the Donkey).

Arts/Crafts Experience

- One of Benjamin Franklin's important inventions was the bifocal lens. Try some bifocal art. Give students a large bifocal glass pattern they can trace around. Then students pick something to draw. They should draw one half normal-sized and one half enlarged (to show how things are viewed from a pair of bifocal lenses).

Values Education Experience

- Benjamin Franklin was known for his quips and words of wisdom: "Dost thou love life? Then do not squander time, for that is the stuff that life is made up of" or "Think what you do when you run in debt; you give to another power over your liberty . . . It is hard for an empty bag to stand upright." Discuss one of these statements and how it applies to students' lives.

Follow-Up/Homework Idea

- Ask students to spot-check their homes for electrical safety (no frayed cords, flammable storage areas, etc.).

Winnie the Pooh Day

January 18

Setting the Stage

- Attach balloons to a Winnie the Pooh bear on the door with a sign that says "Welcome to Pooh Corner!"

- Display student work with a Winnie the Pooh Bear and the caption: "Beary Good Work!"

- Construct a semantic web with facts the students already know about Winnie the Pooh (or other characters in Pooh-related books). Then ask students what they would like to learn about this cuddly bear today.

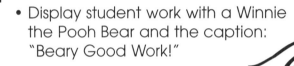

Historical Background

The author of *Winnie the Pooh*, A.A. Milne, was born on this day in 1882.

Literary Exploration

A.A. Milne by Jill C. Wheeler
A.A. Milne: The Man Behind Winnie the Pooh by Ann Thwaite
The House at Pooh Corner by A.A. Milne
Now We Are Six by A.A. Milne
Walt Disney's Winnie the Pooh and Tigger Too by Walt Disney
When We Were Very Young by A.A. Milne
Winnie the Pooh by A.A. Milne

Language Experience

• Have students fold a sheet of paper into fourths and write and illustrate four main events (in sequential order) from one of Pooh's adventures.

Writing Experience

• A.A. Milne gained inspiration for his Winnie the Pooh characters from his son, Christopher Robin and his stuffed animals. Ask students to write adventures about their favorite stuffed animals. See reproducible on page 129.

Math Experience

• Serve up some math in a honey pot. Transform a cookie jar or pot into a "Pooh Honey Pot." Place numbers on small individual pieces of paper inside it. Students stick their hands into the pot, pull out numbers one at a time and add, subtract or multiply them (depending on what they are currently studying.

Music/Dramatic Experience

• Play musical chairs to Kenny Loggins' music, "Return to Pooh Corner."

• Let students act out a favorite scene from one of the Winnie the Pooh stories.

Physical/Sensory Experience

• Winnie the Pooh is known for his love of honey and his need to slim down. Encourage students to help Winnie with a little winter workout (running in place, stretching exercises, sit-ups and push-ups).

Arts/Crafts Experience

• Students will enjoy making Winnie the Pooh figures out of modeling clay.

• Involve fast finishers in drawing a mural of Hundred Acre Wood (where Winnie and his friends live).

Extension Activities

⚠ Use a refrigerator cookie dough mix or make up your favorite sugar cookie recipe for "Pooh Paw Prints." Students flatten out their cookies and make indentations (footprints) in the dough. Bake according to directions.

⚠ Host a Pooh Party and invite students to bring their stuffed animals. What do Pooh Bears like to eat best? Honey! Serve honey on crackers, triangular-shaped pieces of bread or honey-graham crackers!

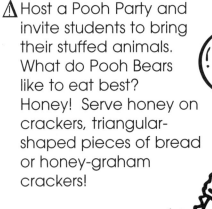

Follow-Up/Homework Idea

• Encourage students to read an A.A. Milne book or watch a Winnie the Pooh video tonight.

Robert E. Lee's Birthday

January 19

Setting the Stage

• Display pictures, books or memorabilia associated with the Civil War.

• Construct a semantic map or web with facts your students already know about the Civil War. Then have them write questions they want answered throughout the activities for the day.

Historical Background

Robert E. Lee was commander in chief of the Confederate Army during the Civil War. He was born on this day in 1807.

Literary Exploration

America's Robert E. Lee by Henry Steele Commager
A Picture Book of Robert E. Lee by David A. Adler
Robert E. Lee by Nathan Aaseng
Robert E. Lee by Marian Cannon
Robert E. Lee by Jack Kavanaugh
Robert E. Lee: A Boy of Old Virginia by Helen Albee Monsell
Robert E. Lee, Brave Leader by Rae Bains
Robert E. Lee, Hero of the South by Charles Parlin Graves
Robert E. Lee: Leader in War and Peace by Carol Greene
Robert E. Lee: The South's Great General by Dan Zadra
Robert E. Lee: Young Confederate by Helen Albee Monsell

Language Experience

• Review the language skills you are currently working on with a relay game of the "Blue" team against the "Gray" team.

Writing Experience

• Have each student write a letter home as a Confederate soldier during the Civil War. See reproducible on page 133.

Math Experience

• Host math relays (with the math concepts you are currently studying). One side of the room can be the South with their leader, Robert E. Lee and the other side can be the North led by Ulysses S. Grant.

Social Studies Experience

• Study the Civil War: the events leading up to it, the issues at stake, the southern states involved, the destruction and the part Robert E. Lee played including his surrender to the North. Robert E. Lee did not believe in slavery or in breaking up the Union, but he felt such loyalty to his native Virginia that he led them into battle anyway. He was so well loved and respected that some southern states observe this day as a legal holiday.

Music/Dramatic Experience

• Divide students into the North and the South and let each side debate their cause (Union and Confederate) with the other.

• Let students role-play the surrender of the Southern army at Appomattox.

Arts/Crafts Experience

• Students can make Confederate flags to hang in the room for the rest of the day.

TLC10466 Copyright © Teaching & Learning Company, Carthage, IL 62321-0010

Inauguration
Day

January 20

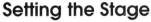

Setting the Stage

• Display pictures or President-related literature to add interest in today's activities.

• Rotate students, giving them the honor of being class president for a certain amount of time today (even 15 minutes of fame is something). Put your desk in the center of the room as part of the "Oval Office" and let student presidents sit there and help you with "executive" decisions throughout the day.

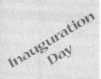

• Construct a semantic web with facts your students already know (or would like to know) about the President and his term of office.

Historical Background

A Presidential Inauguration happens only once every four years, and this is the day set aside for it. Before 1933, Presidents took the oath of office on March 4, then the Twentieth Amendment was passed making January 20th the official day.

Literary Exploration

Arthur Meets the President by Marc Brown
Ask Me Anything About the President by Louis Phillip
The Buck Stops Here by Alice Provensen
Hail to the Chief!: Jokes About the President by Diane Burns
The Look-It-Up Book of Presidents by Wyatt Blassingame
Presidents of the United States by Richard O'Neill and Antonia D. Bryan

Language Experience

• Brainstorm names of Presidents, then let students put the names in alphabetical order or in their order of service.

• Play Clothesline (like the Hangman game). Students try to avoid placing items of clothes on the clothesline by correctly guessing the right letters in a President's name.

Writing Experience

• Have students write what kind of President they would be if they worked in the Oval Office. They should title their papers "If I Were President." See reproducible on page 138.

• Invite students to take their concerns and issues facing our country directly to the top by writing to the Oval office at:

The President
The White House
1600 Pennsylvania Ave.
Washington, D.C. 20500

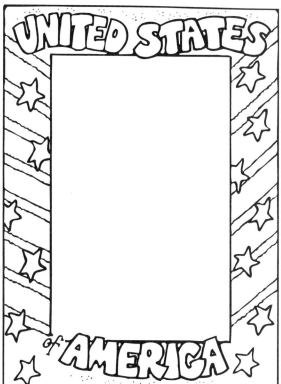

Math Experience

- More than one-and-a-half million visitors tour the White House each year. How many would that average in a single day? Have students average how many visitors come to their homes in a single day. They can tally the results on a bar graph.

Social Studies Experience

- Study the line of Presidents from George Washington down to our current President. Have students make a time line of Presidents and significant events during each presidency.

1789   2000

- Invite interested students to research their favorite Presidents and share their findings with the rest of the class.

Music/Dramatic Experience

- Students can take turns giving inaugural speeches in front of small groups or the rest of the class.

Arts/Crafts Experience

• Students can work together on a giant mural of the President's place of residence, the White House. Have them draw what they think it looks like on the inside as well as the outside.

Extension Activities

• If you decided to choose presidents in your class today, why not lengthen their stay of office? Choose a rotating president and cabinet members: Secretaries of State, Treasury, Defense, Transportation, Energy, Education, Labor, Commerce, Interior, Agriculture, Housing and Urban Development, Health and Human Services, Veterans Affairs and Attorney General. Let students decide on the skills and duties for each. (Example: The Secretary of Energy makes sure the lights are off every time your class leaves the room.) Students can apply for the jobs. Choose a new president and cabinet every month or so.

Follow-Up/Homework Idea

• Ask students to talk to their parents or grandparents about what Presidents of the United States they remember when they were growing up.

Hat Day

January 21

Setting the Stage

• Display all kinds of hats (occupational, protective and decorative) to stimulate interest in the day's activities.

• On a bulletin board display student work surrounded by all kinds of hats with the caption: "HATS off to you!"

• Keep your students' attention by putting on a new hat every hour or so. Invite students to wear their favorite hats today.

• Construct a semantic web with facts your students know about hats and why people wear them. They can write questions about hats they would like to have answered.

Literary Exploration

Aunt Flossie's Hats (And Crab Cakes Later) by Elizabeth Fitzgerald Howard

Away Went the Farmer's Hat by Jane Belk Moncure

Big Pig's Hat by Willy Smax

Caps for Sale by Esphyr Slobodkina

Catch That Hat! by Emma Chichester Clark

Felix's Hat by Catherine Bancroft

The 500 Hats of Bartholemew Cubbins by Dr. Suess

Flower Pot Is Not a Hat by Martha Moffett

A Hat Is So Simple by Jerry Smath

Herman's Hat by George Mendoza

I'm Looking for My Hat by Arthur Speer

Jennie's Hat by Ezra Jack Keats

Keep Your Old Hat by Anna Grossnickle Hines

Look at Me in a Funny Hat by Richard Johnson

Madeline and the Bad Hat by Ludwig Bemelmans

A Man and His Hat by Letitia Parr

Martin's Hats by Joan Blos

"Mr. Smeds and Mr. Spats" a poem from *Where the Sidewalk Ends* by Shel Silverstein

Miss Apple's Hats by Carol Greene

Mr. Momboo's Hat by Ralph Leemis

My Grandfather's Hat by Melanie Scheller

Sebastion Lives in a Hat by Thelma Caterwell

Story Hat by Verna Aardema

This Is a Hat: A Story in Rhyme by Nancy Van Laan

Uncle Lester's Hat by Howie Schnieder

Who Took the Farmer's Hat? by Joan Nodsett

Whose Hat Was That? by Brian Wildsmith

Whose Hat? by Margaret Miller

Language Experience

• Let students brainstorm words that rhyme with *hat*.

Writing Experience

- Let students pick hats off the display table and write adventures about the people they imagine would wear the hats.

Math Experience

- Bring all the hats you gathered into a central area. Let students measure the hats in inches, centimeters, area, perimeter, weigh them on scales, etc.

US NAVY

Science/Health Experience

- Display hats from health and science-related fields (such as a nurse or firefighter would wear). Invite students to figure out which hat belongs to which profession.

Social Studies Experience

- Study the history of hats. How have they changed over time?

- Discuss hats that are worn for religious or cultural reasons around the world. Let students pronounce their names (sombrero, yarmulke, beret).

Music/Dramatic Experience

- Sing the old German folk song, "My Hat It Has Three Corners."

Physical/Sensory Experience

- Host a Hat Parade! Let students parade around the school wearing homemade hats of all kinds!

Arts/Crafts Experience

• Provide students craft materials such as fabric, construction paper, newspaper, felt, sewing tools, odds and ends. Let them be creative and come up with their own wacky headgear!

Extension Activities

• Invite a milliner to come and talk to your class about his or her work.

• If there is a millinery shop nearby, take your class on a field trip to watch how hats are made.

⚠ Give each student a muffin, a craft stick and some frosting. Have them create hats that look "good enough to eat!" Then eat them.

Couch Potato Buster's Day

January 22

Setting the Stage

- Let students make large potatoes cut from brown grocery sacks. They can draw their own faces on the potatoes. Review basic hygiene and grooming tips which they can write on the potato heads. Display them on a bulletin board with the caption: "Keep Yourself A-Peeling!"

- Construct a semantic map or web with facts students know about potatoes. Then ask them to list some things they would like to learn about potatoes today.

Historical Background

The word *potato* comes from an Indian word that Spanish explorers heard as *batatas*. The Spanish brought some of these "batatas" from South America to Florida. After the British invasion of the Spanish colonies in Florida, the "batatas" were taken to their homeland. *Batatas* sounded like *potatoes* to them. The potato grew so well in Ireland, it became its staple crop. Irish settlers brought potatoes with them to America where they have remained popular since the 18th century.

Literary Exploration

Ada Potato by Judith Caseley
Jamie O' Rourke and the Big Potato by Tomie de Paola
The Mouse and the Potato by Thomas Berger
Olav's Potato Field by Jo Tenfjord
One Potato, Two Potato by Mary Lou Colgin
Potatoes, Potatoes by Anita Lobel
The Potato Man by Megan McDonald
The Potato Party and Other Troll Tales by Loreen Leedy
Potato Talk by Ennis Rees
The Tattooed Potato and Other Clues by Ellen Raskin

Language Experience

- Explain that some people are called "couch potatoes" because of endless hours spent in front of the television set. Encourage students not to be "couch potatoes" but to turn off the TV and grab a book or go outside. Challenge students to go for a week without any TV. Encourage them to read and share book reports with the class.

- Brainstorm ways to fix and eat, potatoes: mashed, baked, fried, stuffed, hash browns, French fries, etc.

Writing Experience

- Bring a Mr. Potato Head™ toy to class. Have students write about one of his adventures.

- George Crum, a New York chef, is credited with the invention of the potato chip. After feeling insulted when a customer told him his fried potatoes were too thick, he cut them in paper-thin slices. Instead of complaining about them, the customer loved them! Have students cut potato shapes from brown paper bags and write about their favorite potato dishes on them.

Math Experience

- Review simple fractions with potato sections.

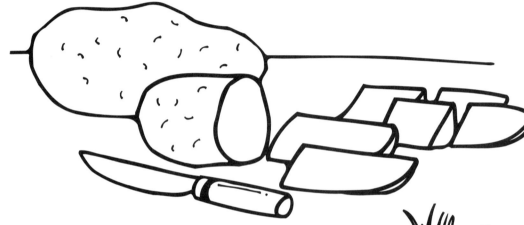

Science/Health Experience

- Study the potato and its ability to actually produce more plants. A potato is technically called a "tuber." It stores food in the form of sugar and starch and grows from the roots of the potato plant. Challenge students to find more interesting potato facts through research.

- Let students grow Potato Heads! They slice off the bottom of a potato and set it upright in a small dish of water. Then they scoop the top of the potato, line the area with cotton batting, add grass seed and keep it watered. Within a week the potato should be sporting a new "do" of green hair. Students can add facial features with cloves (easily stuck into a potato) or buttons that can be glued on.

Social Studies Experience

- Ireland's Great Potato Famine in 1845 was responsible for many Irish people immigrating to America. Have students research more about this famine and how it affected the Irish people.

- Review manners and getting along with others with this fun presentation. Decorate potatoes with markers, fabric and yarn (or use toy potatoes from the Potato Head™ family). Make each one to represent a personality type (the Irra-tater, Agi-tater, Hezi-tater, Dic-tater, etc). Use them to discuss people's personality traits.

Music/Dramatic Experience

- Play an old-fashioned rhyming game of One Potato, Two Potato! Students are divided into manageable groups and sit down in a circle. They form their hands into fists and put their fists in front of them. The leader begins by touching his or her chin and then each fist around the circle with his or her own fist and chanting the following verse (touching a fist with each word):

   "One potato, two potato, three potato, four,
   Five potato, six potato, seven potato, more.
   Y-O-U spells YOU and O-U-T spells OUT."

   At the end of the verse on the word *out* the person whose fist was touched puts that fist behind their back and it is out of the game. As the game progresses, more and more fists are "out" until one is left. That student becomes the new leader for the next round!

Physical/Sensory Experience

- Drag your "couch potatoes" outside (weather permitting) or move desks aside for some physical fitness! Show them a map of the United States (an atlas with road mileage) and invite them to "Race Across America!" Set a goal to run a mile each day (outside or inside) Track student progress from coast to coast. Convert each mile to a certain number of road miles on the map. Draw and cut out a miniature "runner" and pin it to the map to show the progress made. Celebrate when you reach your goal and encourage students to never be "couch potatoes."

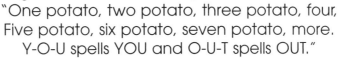

Physical/Sensory Experience continued

- Play Hot Potato Ball! Use a ball or beanbag for the "hot potato." Students sit or stand in a circle. The leader throws the "hot potato" to another student, then turns around with his back to the others. The students quickly pass the "potato" because it is very hot! When the leader yells, "Ouch," whoever is holding the "hot potato" is out of the game. Anyone who drops the "potato" is eliminated. The game continues until one player is left. That person is the new leader.

- Have Potato Sack Races! Get large potato sacks (of heavy burlap) and have students hop across a field in them.

- Have students race while holding a raw potato between their knees. They drop it in a bucket at the end of the line. The first team to fill the bucket with potatoes wins.

Arts/Crafts Experience

- Create "Potato People." Provide potatoes, craft eyes and other items such as fabric, pipe cleaners, yarn, etc. Let students create potato people. Remember that the "eyes" have it! (If you keep them around for a while, the potato people will turn into "monsters" as they grow sprouts.)

⚠ Let students make edible versions of potato people by adding vegetable or fruit features on the potatoes with toothpicks.

Arts/Crafts Experience continued

• Mash potatoes with very little milk and butter. Leave them a little lumpy and let students make potato sculptures. They can add craft sticks or plastic utensils. The sculptures can be brushed with egg white and broiled slightly for a glossy finish. (Make sure the potatoes are cool before using them.)

• Let students make potato prints. Provide potato halves with various designs cut on the ends. Students dip the potato halves in paint or ink to create interesting designs on paper.

Extension Activities

⚠ Host a Potato Bar! Bake potatoes and provide a variety of toppings for students to choose from. You can also serve potato rolls.

⚠ Potato boats are fun to make and eat. After cutting baked potatoes in half, scoop out the inside but leave the shell of the potato skin. Mash the potatoes, add sour cream or cheese and replace the mixture back into the potato shell. Let each student add a small "sail" made from a cheese slice on a toothpick.

Follow-Up/Homework Idea

• Encourage students to make potatoes to eat with their families tonight.

National Handwriting Day

January 23

Setting the Stage

- If you teach younger students, display large words around the room for them to read. They need many opportunities to read and relate words to their environment. Your classroom can be filled with words such as *computer, window, desk* and *clock*. This will help students learn to read and write and to transfer the world of words into something they can see and relate to on a daily basis.

Setting the Stage continued

• Provide new pencils and plenty of writing paper for today's activities. Introduce yourself as "Dr. B.T. FullRiting." Explain that as a doctor your number one pet peeve is careless handwriting and your job today will be to cure everyone in class of their handwriting diseases! Model silly handwriting diseases such as "King Kongosis" (letters too large) or "Claustrophobis" (letters squished together). Tell the class you will be on the alert for those who have "sick" handwriting. Let them write and practice alleviating their "diseases." Walk around and model correct handwriting for each one. As students show that their handwriting is "cured" of disease, give each a certificate for a "Healthy Handwriting Bill of Health." See certificate on page 154.

Historical Background

The first signer of the Declaration of Independence, John Hancock, was born on this day in 1737. He signed his name larger than usual to make sure the King of England could see it.

Literary Exploration

John Hancock by Susan Lee
John Hancock: First Signer of Declaration by Dennis B. Fradin
Muggie Maggie by Beverly Cleary
Will You Sign Here, John Hancock? by Jean Fritz

Language Experience

- Brainstorm various ways to write without a pencil.

Writing Experience

- Give students a chance to write letters in their best handwriting to other students or adults in your school.

Math Experience

- Let students practice their handwriting by writing a math story problem for other students to solve.

Social Studies Experience

- Study the life of John Hancock and the events leading up to his signing of the Declaration of Independence. He was a bold advocate of America's independence and he wanted to make sure King George (in England) could read Hancock's name without his spectacles!

- In ancient times, most people did not know how to write, so they paid scribes to do written work for them. Have your students "hire" (with play money) one another for the day's writing. Make sure each student gets a chance to be a scribe for another and that the work is "worthy" of scribe wages.

Music/Dramatic Experience

- Let students act out the signing of the Declaration of Independence.

Physical/Sensory Experience

• Students can practice their best handwriting in colored chalk on school sidewalks. Let them check one another's work.

• Cook up a pot of spaghetti, then when it's cool students can shape the noodles into letters of their names in cursive.

Arts/Crafts Experience

• Let students try making ink with 1/2 cup of ripe berries (any kind), 1/2 teaspoon of vinegar and 1/2 teaspoon of salt. They can crush the berries with a wooden spoon against a metal strainer so the juice separates from the pulp. Then they add the vinegar and salt, stir the mixture and add water to get the right consistency. Provide feathers to be used as "quill pens" which they dip into the ink to write. Have students wear smocks or old shirts to keep from staining their school clothes.

• Students can make chalkboard "slates" for their very best handwriting. Provide black construction paper and craft sticks (for the "edges" of the slate boards). Have them write the phrase from the Declaration of Independence, "All men are created equal," on the slate, then frame it with craft sticks glued around the edges.

Values Education Experience

• Discuss what it means to put your signature on a document. Explain that one's good name and honor are associated with a personal signature. (Sometimes, a person's signature is referred to as a "John Hancock.") Explain that a document with a signature on it is considered legally binding, so we need to be careful what we sign.

Follow-Up/Homework Idea

• Ask students to show parents their very best handwriting samples.

Healthy Handwriting

Bill of Health

Awarded to:

Teacher

Gold Fever Day

January 24

Setting the Stage

• Today you're on the hunt for the Mother Lode! Apples and Spice Potpourri Sachets (little packets containing sweet-smelling potpourri) look like gold "nuggets" and will make a great display surrounded by pictures and gold-related literature.

• Construct a semantic map or web with facts your students know (or would like to know) about gold.

Historical Background

Gold was discovered at Sutter's Mill on this day in 1848. James Marshal found gold while building a sawmill near Sacramento, California. Thousands of gold-seekers rushed to the area to try to get "rich quick." This period of time became known as the Gold Rush of 1848.

Literary Exploration

The California Gold Rush by May Vonge McNeer
Gold Fever by A.I. Lak
Salt Is Better Than Gold by Stepan Zavrel
The Story of the Gold at Sutter's Mill by Conrad R. Stein

Language Experience

• Create excitement by "digging" for compound words (or other grammatical features) in a story.

Writing Experience

• Students can write for information about gold prospecting by writing to:
U.S. Department of the Interior
  Geological Survey
12201 Sunrise Valley Drive
Reston, VA 20192

• See reproducible on page 158.

Math Experience

• Write math problems (2 + 8 =) or (3 x 5 =) on paper "nugget" shapes and hide them around the room. Have students go on a gold-digger's hunt to find them and solve them. Then they can trade the nuggets they found with one another.

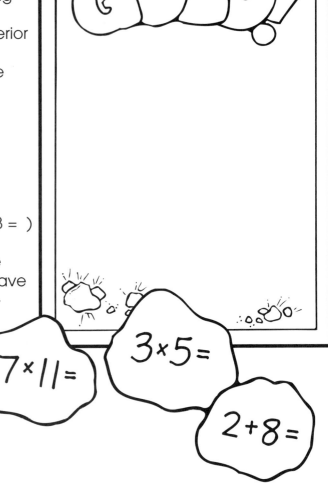

$7 \times 11 =$

$3 \times 5 =$

$2 + 8 =$

Social Studies Experience

• Study the Gold Rush and mark it on a class time line.

Music/Dramatic Experience

• Try Prospector Pantomiming. Brainstorm various pantomiming actions. Write each one on a slip of paper. Place them in a pie tin. Students shake the pie tin and choose a slip of paper. They read the slip and perform the action. The other students try to guess what it is.

Physical/Sensory Experience

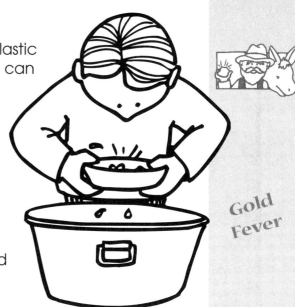

- Have a scavenger or treasure hunt! Fill a plastic tub with sand and add pennies so students can "pan for gold."

- Play the Hotter . . . Colder game! Students try to find a hidden object—"gold." As the searcher gets closer, the class chants "hotter" and "colder" as he or she gets farther from the object, until it is located.

- Give students butterscotch cookies and let them use, toothpicks to "excavate" for gold (butterscotch chips).

Arts/Crafts Experience

- Students can work together on a giant mural of the California Gold Rush showing settlers panning for gold.

Extension Activities

- Invite a gemologist to talk to your class about working with gem stones.

- If your area hosts a gem and mineral show, it would be a great field trip for your class.

⚠ Serve "Gold-Digger Sundaes." Provide tin pans (from pot pies) filled with Tin-Roof Ice Cream. Students can "dig" for gold nuggets (peanuts). Serve water in mason jars (to wash it all down).

⚠ For a quick Gold Fever treat, most grocery stores sell foil-covered "nugget" candies or Pepperidge Farm Geneva Cookies™ (choco-late "dirt" with pecan "gold").

Values Education Experience

- Discuss how people "search" for things (happiness, friendship, etc.) that are much more lasting than gold or silver. Ask students where happiness can be found.

Winter Olympic Games Day

January 25

Setting the Stage

- Display pictures of Winter Olympic events (ice skating, speed skating, ice hockey, luge, biathlon, bobsledding, downhill skiing, slalom, giant slalom, ski jumping and cross-country skiing).

- Construct a semantic map with everything your students know (or would like to know) about the Winter Olympic Games to help you plan today's learning activities.

Historical Background

Although not officially established until 1928, it is generally recognized that the first Winter Olympic Games were held on this day in Chamonix, France, in 1924.

Literary Exploration

Sledding by Elizabeth Winthrop
Winter Olympics by Caroline Arnold
Winter Olympics by Frank Litsky
Winter Olympics by Jack Harris
Winter Olympics by Julian May

Language Experience

- Brainstorm Winter Olympic events, then have students alphabetize them.

- Create a Venn diagram together showing the similarities and differences between the Summer and Winter Olympic Games.

Writing Experience

- Ask students if they had the opportunity to participate in any winter sporting event, what would it be and why. Have them write about their choices. See reproducible on page 162.

Math Experience

- Let students survey other students about their favorite winter sports activities. They can tally the results and add the information on a class bar graph.

Science/Health Experience

- Review winter sports safety.

Social Studies Experience
• Study the history of the Winter Olympic Games.

Music/Dramatic Experience
• Students will enjoy pantomiming Olympic events for other students to guess.

Physical/Sensory Experience
• Take your class outside to participate in their own version of the Winter Olympic Games.

Arts/Crafts Experience
• Provide sports magazines for students to cut out pictures to make a winter sports collage.

Extension Activities
• Invite someone interested in the Winter Olympic Games to share information with your class.

Follow-Up/Homework Idea
• Challenge students to involve their family members in some winter sports such as sledding, skating or snowball fighting.

Michigan Statehood Day

January 26

Setting the Stage

- Michigan was the first state to manufacture cars. Henry Ford believed every family should be able to afford a car, but cars were expensive. Ford developed assembly-line manufacturing. Having each assembly line worker concentrate on only one area of car production enabled his company to make more cars at a lower cost. Cars could be turned out at a much faster rate. Display pictures of cars, toy cars, model cars and automobile-related literature beneath a map of Michigan.

- Construct a semantic web with facts your students know (or would like to know) about the state of Michigan.

Historical Background
Michigan became the 26th state on this day in 1837.

Literary Exploration
America the Beautiful: Michigan by Conrad Stein
Michigan by Martin Hintz
Michigan by Karen Sirvaitis
Michigan by Kathleen Thompson
Michigan in Words and Pictures by Dennis B. Fradin

Writing Experience
- Battle Creek, Michigan, makes more cereal than any other city in the world! Let students study a few cereal boxes to see, the advertisements and the ingredients and how it is packaged. Then have them create new cereals (with packaging advertisements and ingredients listed).

Math Experience

- Discuss the fact that although the first cars were made in America, many cars are now produced outside the U.S. Let students estimate how many cars in the school parking lot are American-made and how many are foreign. Take them to the school parking lot (with adult helpers for safety). How many American-made cars are there? How many foreign? Take the information back to your class to make a class bar graph.

- While your class is in the parking lot, have them look at license plates. Challenge them to add the numbers on each license plate. They can find out which license plate has the smallest total number and which has the largest.

Science/Health Experience

- Automobile safety is important. Review car safety rules (such as wearing seat belts or not distracting the driver).

Social Studies Experience

- Study Michigan and its unique characteristics.

- Challenge students to do some research to find out what car manufacturers are still in Michigan.

Music/Dramatic Experience

• Let students pretend to be salesmen and "sell" a car or a new kind of cereal.

Physical/Sensory Experience

• Provide small toy cars and let students create a city with streets drawn on butcher paper.

Arts/Crafts Experience

• Salt is the chief product of the state of Michigan. Show students how to make a "salt" dough relief map of this great state!

> **Salt Dough**
> 2 c. flour
> 1 c. salt
> 2 T. oil
> Add water to the desired consistency in order to shape and mold in place. Bake in a 350°F oven for one hour. Paint with tempera.

• Students can make their own driving or learner's permits. Tell them if they are guilty of any infraction during the day they will have their learner's permit revoked. See reproducibles on page 168.

Learner's Permit

Guymon
Last Name

Rachel
First Name

2-28-99
Date

Self-Portrait

Arts/Crafts Experience continued

• Have students think of license plate messages with approximately seven or eight letters to describe themselves (Example: IAMSMART). See reproducible on page 169.

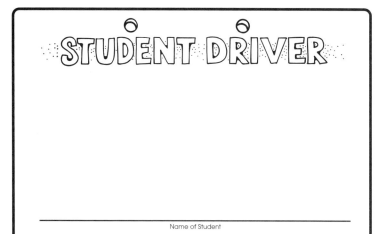

STUDENT DRIVER

_____
Name of Student

• Provide magazines for students to cut out pictures of all types of automobiles to make a collage.

Extension Activities

⚠ Let students make "assembly-line" snacks. Line up ingredients and have each student add one thing until the snack is ready to eat.

• If you live near an automobile factory or a car lot, schedule your class for a visit.

Follow-Up/Homework Idea

• Encourage students to make sure their families are buckled up safely when in the car.

Learner's Permit

Last Name _____

First Name _____

Date _____

Self-Portrait

Learner's Permit

Last Name _____

First Name _____

Date _____

Self-Portrait

Learner's Permit

Last Name _____

First Name _____

Date _____

Self-Portrait

Learner's Permit

Last Name _____

First Name _____

Date _____

Self-Portrait

STUDENT DRIVER

Name of Student

Mad Hatter Day

January 27

Setting the Stage
• Display *Alice in Wonderland* memorabilia and Lewis Carroll's children's books.

Historical Background
Lewis Carroll, the English author of the *Alice in Wonderland* series, was born on this day in 1832.

170

Literary Exploration

Alice's Adventures in Wonderland by Lewis Carroll
The Humorous Verse of Lewis Carroll by Lewis Carroll
Illustrated Lewis Carroll by Lewis Carroll
Lewis Carroll, Author of Alice's Adventure in Wonderland by Lewis Carroll
Poems of Lewis Carroll by Lewis Carroll
Through the Looking Glass by Lewis Carroll

Language Experience

• Have students review and sequence the events in *Alice in Wonderland*.

• Play Clothesline (a variation of the Hangman game) with Lewis Carroll's real name (Charles Lutwidge Dodgson). Students try to avoid adding clothes to the line by guessing the correct letters of his name.

Math Experience

• Tweedledee and Tweedledum never had this much fun! Pair up students to do partner math. One student (Tweedledee) does half of the math problems today and the other (Tweedledum) checks the work for correct answers. Then they switch jobs for the second half.

Social Studies Experience

• Invite students to research the life of Lewis Carroll and share the information with the class.

Music/Dramatic Experience

- Divide students into groups and let them act out scenes from *Alice in Wonderland*.

Physical/Sensory Experience

- Let students play a game of croquet with a designated "Queen of Hearts."

Arts/Crafts Experience

- Let students draw or paint pictures of their own personal "Wonderlands."

Extension Activities

⚠ Mix up your favorite sugar cookie recipe or use refrigerator cookie dough. Let students create heart cookies using heart-shaped cookie cutters. They can dress up fancy as if going to a Mad Hatter Party and eat the cookies and drink punch.

Emmy Award Day

January 28

Setting the Stage
- Construct a semantic map or web with facts your students know (or would like to know) about television to help you plan activities for the day.

Historical Background

The first television Emmy Awards were given on this day in 1948.

Language Experience
- Let students say their favorite television programs, then put them in alphabetical order.

Writing Experience

• Divide students into cooperative groups and let them write scripts for television shows.

For a quick, easy snack, try . . .

Math Experience

• Let students survey others about their favorite TV programs. They can tally the results and add them to a class bar graph.

Science/Health Experience

• Students will enjoy making up commercials to advertise healthy foods to eat.

• Study how television works. Younger children are often fascinated by how the pictures and sounds come out of a box.

Social Studies Experience

• Learn about the history of television. Discuss how it has changed in the last 50 plus years.

Music/Dramatic Experience

• Use a video camera to tape students performing their group television shows and commercials (see above).

• Let your class debate the pros and cons of television.

174

Arts/Crafts Experience
- Let students decorate "sets" (scenery and props) for their television shows. (See "Music/Dramatic Experience" on page 174).

Extension Activities
- Host an Emmy Awards show! After students have performed their television shows, ask the class (or a panel of judges) to vote for Emmy Awards. Every group should win in some category (Most Creative, Best Script, Best Acting, etc.). Then at the awards show, use a video camera to "pan" the audience for winner responses as in a real Emmy Awards show. Tape the winners giving acceptance speeches. Show these to the class later for a good laugh!

⚠ Eat "TV dinners" together for lunch in your room.

- Visit a local television station to watch how a program is televised.

- Invite someone from a local television station to come and speak to your class.

Values Education Experience
- Discuss the value of moderation when watching TV. Caution against becoming a TV "couch potato."

Follow-Up/Homework Idea
- Invite students to watch a favorite television show with their families.

Pasta Party Day

January 29

Setting the Stage
• Display packages of various types of pasta and noodles.

• Construct a semantic map or web with facts your students know (or would like to know) about noodles and pasta.

Literary Exploration
All of Our Noses Are Here, and Other Noodle Tales by Alvin Schwartz
Noodle by Munro Leaf
Pasta by Kate Schwartz
Strega Nona: An Old Tale by Tomie de Paola
There Is a Carrot in My Ear and Other Noodle Tales by Alvin Schwartz
Upside Down Day by Mike Thaler

Language Experience
• List types of pasta (orzo, ditalini, gemeli, penne, mafalda, mostaccioli, fettuccine, bow tie, linguine, stellini, vermicelli, cavatelli, rotelli, rigatoni, fusilli, manicotti, ziti and macaroni). Let students put them in alphabetical order.

Writing Experience

- Let students write their favorite pasta recipes to be compiled into a class Pasta Cookbook. See reproducibles on page 179.

- Try Punctuation Pasta. Have students print sentences in large letters and use noodles for punctuation marks.

Math Experience

- Let students use pasta noodles as math manipulatives for counting, adding and subtracting during math today.

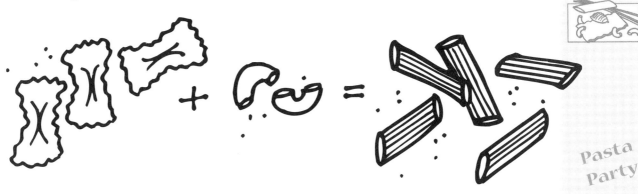

- Pasta and noodles are fun to measure in length and weight.

- Have students sort and graph various colors, shapes and sizes of pasta.

Music/Dramatic Experience
• Have students "advertise" new types of pasta. They can pretend to be in television commercials.

Arts/Crafts Experience
• Let students make collages out of dry pasta noodles, or they can thread pasta on string to make "Noodle Necklaces."

• Students can dip yarn in red tempera paint and arrange it around pictures of themselves as if they are eating "spaghetti."

Extension Activities
• If you live near a pasta factory, take a class field trip to see how pasta is made.

• Many people make their own noodles at home. Invite a "noodle maker" to come and show your class how to make homemade noodles.

⚠ Have a Pasta Tasting Party! Have students bring all kinds of pasta and noodles and have a little taste of each.

Follow-Up/Homework Idea
• Encourage students to eat pasta with their families.

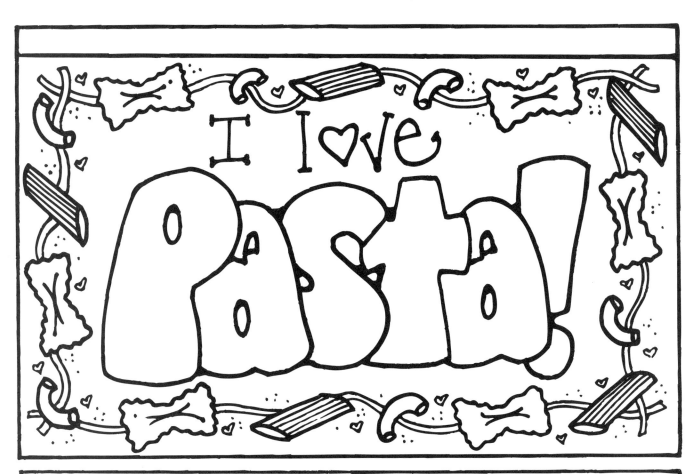

FDR Day

January 30

Setting the Stage

- Display pictures of the Great Depression around books about Franklin Delano Roosevelt or the Great Depression.

- Construct a semantic map or web with facts your students know about the Depression. Then ask them to list questions they would like answered today.

Historical Background

Franklin Delano Roosevelt (FDR) was the 32nd President of the United States. He was born on this day in 1882. Roosevelt overcame many personal struggles including polio at the height of his career. He also had to face enormous country and world-wide problems, serving during our country's worst economic depression and World War II.

32 PRESIDENT

Literary Exploration

Franklin Delano Roosevelt by Bob Italia

Franklin Delano Roosevelt and the New Deal by Sharon Shebar

Franklin Delano Roosevelt, Gallant President by Barbara Silberdick Feinberg

Franklin Delano Roosevelt: The People's President by John W. Selfridge

Franklin Delano Roosevelt: Thirty-Second President of the United States by Alice Osinski

Language Experience

- Challenge students to see how many words they can make with the letters in *Franklin Delano Roosevelt*.

Writing Experience

- FDR made an important speech known as "The Four Freedoms Speech." In it he discussed four essential freedoms: speech and worship and freedom from want and fear. Have students write about these four freedoms, about one freedom in greater detail or about another freedom. See reproducible on page 183.

Social Studies Experience

• Study the period known as the Great Depression. Have students research the events that triggered it, its devastating effect on America and how FDR helped America get back on her feet again with the New Deal.

• Study Roosevelt's presidential administration.

FDR

Extension Activities

• Invite an older person who lived through the Great Depression to tell your students about it. Ask him or her to explain how people were able to survive (physically and emotionally) during this difficult period of history.

FDR

Values Education Experience

• Discuss what Franklin Roosevelt may have meant when he said, "The only thing we have to fear is fear itself." Ask students to share their fears and tell how they overcame them.

FDR

Chinese New Year

January 31

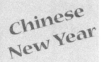

Setting the Stage

• Gung Hay Fat Choy! Happy Chinese New Year! Celebrate the day with some Chinese traditions. Display pictures, Chinese-related literature, fans, lanterns, etc. Put a sign on the door that says "Welcome to China!" or "Gung Hay Fat Choy." Use some Chinese characters. Wear a Chinese silk robe or a robe from home with a piece of material tied around the waist for a cummerbund and a straw hat and thongs. Ask students to remove their shoes at the door.

• Construct a semantic map or web with facts your students know (or would like to know) about the Chinese New Year to help you plan today's learning activities.

Historical Background

Chinese New Year celebrations are held in late January or early February, depending on the lunar calendar. Prior to their celebration, Chinese families thoroughly clean their homes, buy new clothes and pay off all debts to begin the New Year as "new" as possible. Traditionally people celebrate their birthdays and turn a year older at the New Year.   Be sure and tell everyone "Happy Birthday" today! Friends and family gather together to eat special holiday food and visit with one another. Children are given gifts of fruit and red envelopes that contain money. Parades are led by huge Chinese silk and paper dragons (the Chinese symbol of strength and power), to scare away evil spirits.

Chinese
New Year

Chinese
New Year

Chinese
New Year

Literary Exploration

Chinese Brush Painting for Beginners by Vickey Aubrey
Chinese New Year by Tricia Brown
Chinese New Year by Hou-tien Cheng
Chinese New Year by Dianne MacMillan
Chinese New Year's Dragon by Rachel Sing
A Chinese Zoo: Fables and Proverbs by Demi
Dragon Kites and Dragonflies by Demi
The Emperor and the Kite by Jane Yolen
Five Chinese Brothers by Claire Hughet Bishop and Kurt Wiese
Gung Hay Fat Choy by June Behrens
Lion Dancer: Ernie Wan's Chinese New Year by Kate Waters and
    Madeline Slovenz-Low
Lon Po Po: A Red-Riding Hood Story from China by Ed Young
Red Eggs and Dragon Boats: Celebrating Chinese Festivals by Carol
    Stepanchuk
The Seven Chinese Brothers by Margaret Mahy
Yeh-Shen: A Cinderella Story from China by Ai-Ling Louie

Writing Experience

- Each Chinese New Year is named after one of 12 different animals: dragon, snake, rat, horse, ox, tiger, dog, boar, rooster, monkey, ram, rabbit. Provide a Chinese calendar which tells which animal's year you were born in. Have students write why they think they were born in their particular Chinese New Year. Invite them to be silly and not take themselves (or their Chinese New Year animals) too seriously. See reproducible on page 191.

- Because China is so heavily populated, each family is asked to have only one child. Have your students write about the pros and cons of being an only child.

- Hand out fortune cookies you have made (see the recipe on page 190). Also hand out strips of white paper and have students write some new fortunes for the coming year.

Social Studies Experience

• Study Chinese New Year traditions.

• Invite students to research China, the most heavily populated country in the world. Let them share their findings with the class.

Music/Dramatic Experience

• Check out Chinese music from a local library and play it during class. Let students make up their own dances to the music.

Math Experience

• Measure the dimensions of a Chinese dragon.

• In China during the New Year celebration, families display a "money tree" which symbolizes a year of prosperity to come. Let your class make a money tree by putting a dead branch in a wide vase. They can hang paper coins on the branches. Fast finishers can add coins on a particular branch, then use math skills to determine which branch has the most or least amount of money.

• Let students make tangrams (ancient Chinese puzzles) by cutting angular lines from a square piece of paper. They can rearrange the shapes to make animals or pictures.

Physical/Sensory Experience

- If your class decides to make a Chinese dragon, be sure and have a Chinese dragon parade through the hallways or around your school.

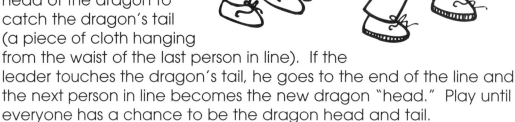

- Play Catch the Dragon's Tail. Students line up (like a long dragon) and hold on to each other's shoulders. The head of the dragon (leader) tries to run around the playing area (with others hanging on) twisting and turning (as a Chinese dragon would). The object is for the head of the dragon to catch the dragon's tail (a piece of cloth hanging from the waist of the last person in line). If the leader touches the dragon's tail, he goes to the end of the line and the next person in line becomes the new dragon "head." Play until everyone has a chance to be the dragon head and tail.

- Have a "Chinese Egg Roll." Divide students into teams and line them up. Give the first person on each team a blown-up balloon and a pair of chopsticks. They try to "prod" the "egg roll" along a path with the chopsticks without breaking the balloon. When the first person reaches his goal, he goes to the end of the line and the next person takes the balloon and continues. The first team to finish wins.

Arts/Crafts Experience

- Teach new art techniques from *Chinese Brush Painting for Beginners* by Vickey Aubrey. Students can try new brush strokes or Chinese characters using black tempera paint on red paper. Hang the completed pieces for decorative banners.

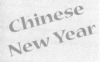
TLC10466 Copyright © Teaching & Learning Company, Carthage, IL 62321-0010

Arts/Crafts Experience continued

- On the third day of the Chinese New Year celebration a Feast of Lanterns is held. Families hang up lanterns of all sizes, shapes and colors. Students can make their own colorful lanterns by folding 9" x 12" sheets of construction paper in half (lengthwise). Then, beginning on the fold-side, they cut slits across the paper, stopping about an inch from the edge. When they unfold, "fan" it out, they have lantern shapes. They can add paper handles and hang them around the room or from the ceiling.

- Students can make miniature dragons by decorating paper plates to look like dragons' heads, then attaching craft sticks for handles. They can hold the dragon "masks," in front of their faces during the dragon parade.

- Have students cut out circles to make Chinese hats. They each cut a slit halfway up the center of the circle and pull the ends together to form a cone shape wide enough to fit his or her head. After they overlap the ends and staple them together, they can decorate the hats with markers, crayons, glitter and sequins. They punch holes on the sides and thread ribbon through the holes to hold the hats on their heads.

Extension Activities

⚠ Host an Oriental Festival! Let students eat Chinese foods with chopsticks. Serve apples and mandarin oranges (red and orange are considered good luck for the Chinese), rice and noodles. Be sure to include fortune cookies. Invite a Chinese guest or someone who can share information about this interesting country. As a culminating activity, have a Dragon Parade! Look for interesting ideas and recipes in the book, *Red Eggs and Dragon Boats: Celebrating Chinese Festivals* by Carol Stepanchuk.

Chinese
New Year

Chinese
New Year

Chinese
New Year

Chinese
New Year

Extension Activities continued

⚠ Make homemade fortune cookies.

Fortune Cookies
Mix: 1 cup (softened) margarine
1/2 cup sugar
4 egg whites

Add the following to the mixture to form a ball of dough:
2 1/2 tablespoons vanilla
3 1/4 cups flour
1/2 teaspoon baking powder

On a lightly floured surface, roll out the dough to about 1/8" thick. Using a round metal cookie cutter, cut the dough into circles. Fortunes (made from thin strips of paper) can be laid on one side of each circle of dough. Then fold the other side over the bottom half and pinch the edges together. Bake on a cookie sheet in a 425°F oven for about 10 minutes until lightly browned.

⚠ Make Chinese New Year Cookies! Melt a package of chocolate chips and mix with a three-ounce can of Chinese noodles and 1/2 cup of salted peanuts. Spoon onto wax paper and chill.

Values Education Experience

• Teach students to have an appreciation for all cultures. Discuss interesting facets of Chinese life and the unique contributions the Chinese make to the world with their delicious food, unique music and art.

Follow-Up/Homework Idea

• Encourage students to ask their parents to have Chinese food for dinner tonight.

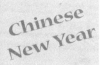